Richard Deiss
Nick Snipes

AF198945

Grand Central Terminal and the station at the end of the world

Short stories about 222 train stations of the Americas, from Alaska to the Land of Fire

<u>Address of the Authors:</u>
Machnowerstr. 65, D-14165 Berlin
Email: richard.deiss@gmail.com
          nick818ns@yahoo.com

Comments are welcome and will be considered in the next edition.

Cover page: Philadelphia 30th Street Station
Inside cover page: New York Grand Central Terminal

Herstellung und Verlag: BoD- Books on Demand, Norderstedt,
Zweite Englischsprachige Ausgabe 2020, Originalausgabe
Second English language edition 2020

The content of the book represents the private opinion of the author.

Printed in Germany

ISBN   978-3-751-9490-19

Bibliografische Information der Deutschen Nationalbibliothek
Die Deutsche Nationalbibliothek verzeichnet diese Publikation in
der Deutschen Nationalbibliografie; detaillierte bibliografische
Daten sind im Internet über http://dnb.d-nb.de abrufbar

Contents

4. South America 106

Annex

Foreword

In summer 2007 I published the paperback Palace of a Thousand Winds and Gooseberry Station, which contained small stories, interesting facts, and anecdotes about 200 train stations worldwide. Over the course of time, more anecdotes accumulated, so in 2008 I published a new edition with 20 more stations, and in early 2009 I finally published a second volume, 'The Gingerbread Station at the End of the World' with 200 anecdotes about train stations outside Europe.

But since there are many anecdotes, especially about the United States, there was a need for a separate volume on America to accommodate all the stories.

After a first edition in summer 2009, an expanded second edition in October 2009, third and fourth editions 2011 and 2013, this is the first English language version (revised by Nick Snipes) of a slightly changed, updated sixth edition.

This book contains anecdotes and facts about over 200 American train stations (half of which are in the United States). It begins in Alaska on a north-south tour, then covers Canadian stations, returns to the US in the northeast and works its way through Mexico, Central America, Brazil, and the Andean countries to Tierra del Fuego at the 'end of the world'. Stories in which well-known personalities occur are marked by a circle ⊙.

A new edition is planned every two years. Hints for other interesting stories and facts about overseas train stations are therefore always welcome.

Berlin, June 2020

Richard Deiss and Nick Snipes

1. Canada and Alaska

The railroad in Canada and Alaska

North America was once the world's leading region in rail transport. Half of all rails around the world, around 500,000 km, were located here; today it comprises only a quarter of all rails. While almost half of the rail network in the United States has been shut down since 1920, Canada has lost only 20,000 of its 70,000 km of track. Nevertheless, in Canada today, rail passenger transport - with a transport performance of around 2 billion passenger-kilometers - plays only a minor role because the population density is low, the distances are simply too great for the train, and more suitable for airplanes. Existing long-distance trains are used primarily for tourism; besides, there is only significant local transport in the metropolitan areas. Accordingly, only train stations in the area of metropolitan rail transport such as Toronto or Montreal are well frequented. The stations are operated by Via Rail, a state-owned railway company that was created in 1978 by separating loss-making passenger traffic from the two major railway companies, Canadian Pacific, and Canadian National Railway.

By contrast, the railroad in Canada is still an important mode of transport in freight transport. Rail freight transport in tonne-kilometers is four times the transport performance provided in Germany. This puts Canada in fifth place worldwide.

In Alaska, railway lines were built late and primarily through government initiatives. Due to the tax revenue from oil production, there is enough money today to maintain the small rail network including the stations and to operate it by the state. The state-owned Alaska Railroad, which owns the rail infrastructure, describes itself as the 'last integrated railroad in North America', i.e. one that operates passenger and freight transport.

1.1 Alaska

⊙ Nenana and the serum

In January 1925, there was a great calamity in the port city of Nome, with its isolated location on the west coast of Alaska. A diphtheria epidemic broke out and this particularly threatened the Eskimo children because they lacked the necessary immunity. Life-saving serum was urgently needed. But how should you get this to Nome? The port of Nome was icy in January and not accessible by ship and there were no roads to Nome. Alaska also had only two transport planes at the time, both of which had never been used in winter. In desperation, they resorted to a combination of rail and sled dog transport. The serum was brought by train from Anchorage to Nenana, a small train station in the interior of Alaska about 60 kilometers west of Fairbanks. From here it was still almost 1000 km to the west coast city of Nome. This route was to be covered with sled dogs on the Iditarod Trail. On January 27, 1925, a dog sled train set out from Nenana station, where the serum was received, to cross the winter hell of Alaska. In total, more than 100 dogs were used. It was thanks to the experienced Norwegian sled dog leader Gunnar Kaasen and his persistent lead dog Balto that the sled dog train arrived in Nome on February 2nd at 5:30 am. Kaasen and his dog became famous, and a bronze statue was built for Balto in New York's Central Park. A Disney film about the events called Balto was also later produced.

Today, the Iditarod dog sled race from Willow to Nome over a longer distance (1868 km) recreates the race over the trail every year in March

1.2 Canada

Craigellachie and 'the Last Spike'

On November 7, 1885, in Craigellachie, British Columbia, the last rail nail was struck into the transcontinental rail link of the Canadian Pacific Railway. Trains stop there today specifically for tourists. However, it wasn't originally the last nail. The railroad financier Donald Smith bent the initial nail on the first hit, so he had to try again with a new one. Additionally, his nail was soon removed - it was given to the son of the patent office president - and replaced by a third to discourage souvenir hunters.

Jumbo and the train

The city of St. Thomas, which was connected to the railway in 1856 and whose current station was built in 1871-1873, was once an important railway hub in the Canadian province of Ontario. 26 different railway companies have served this station over the years and St. Thomas was temporarily considered the Railway Capital of Canada. Since 1985, the statue of the elephant Jumbo stands at the station.

Jumbo was the name of a very large African elephant who was born in French Africa in 1861, imported from a French zoo, and then given to the London Zoo in 1865. The London zookeepers gave it the name Jumbo, which is probably derived from the Swahili jambo (hello). In 1882, the elephant was finally sent to the P. T. Barnum circus company. Barnum made a lot of advertising for the mighty elephant Jumbo, and as a result, jumbo soon stood for big, huge. For example, the Boeing 747 was later also called the Jumbo Jet. But there was something stronger than jumbo. On September 15, 1885, Jumbo died when he tried to save a baby elephant on the tracks of the St. Thomas train station whilst overlooking a locomotive that was approaching. The baby elephant survived, by the way, but had broken a leg and was therefore put to sleep. Jumbo died at the scene of the accident. The circus Barnum had the elephant stuffed and gave it to Tufts University in the USA, wherein 1975 a fire destroyed the taxidermic animal. In 1985, a hundred years after the death of the elephant, a life-size monument was erected at the St. Thomas train station.

St. Thomas' big train station

But even without the elephant, the St. Thomas train station is something special. When it was completed in 1873, the local newspaper wrote:

"As far as the architectural substance and solidity, the value in use of the interior layout and the dimensions are concerned, there is no passenger station in Canada, but at most in New York and Chicago, which is comparable to that of the Canada Southern society in St. Thomas. "

400,000 bricks were installed in the over 100 m long station building. Today, the disused railway station needs repair and a local association has been founded to collect donations for its renovation and to restore the original condition of the long building block, which today lacks the typical canopy roof.

Ottawa Union Station

When Union Station was designed in Ottawa in 1908, numerous ideas were copied from the Pennsylvania station in New York, which was then under construction. The Penn Station waiting room, which was modeled on the Roman Baths of Caracalla, was simply copied on a scale of 1: 2. As in New York, the building was provided with hollow Corinthian columns on the outside (but not on all sides). In 1956, however, the Roman-style dome was removed in favor of a flat roof, and in 1966 the station was completely shut down. The tracks that run along the Rideau Canal, where the train station is located, were also dismantled because the canal bank became the promenade. The canal is now even on the UNESCO World Heritage List. The former Union Station is now a government conference center. A newly built modernist metal construction on the outskirts of the city, which was awarded an architecture prize in 1967 yet is essentially uncomfortable - became the long-distance train station.

Halifax's disaster

The architects of Ottawa's Union Station also designed the new Halifax station. The city's old train station was destroyed in 1917 in the worst disaster in Canadian history. In December 1917, a French frigate loaded with explosives collided with a Norwegian steamship in the city's port. This attracted numerous spectators. At the same time, a sailor rushed into the office of the railway dispatcher Vincent Coleman and warned of an impending huge explosion. Instead of getting to safety, Coleman telegraphed an incoming train that had 700 passengers on board. The passengers were saved, but Coleman, like 2,000 others, was killed in the explosion. He is considered a hero in Canada ever since.

⊙ Saskatoon - the Prime Minister and the newspaper

On the morning of July 29, 1910, the Canadian Prime Minister Sir Wilfried Laurier (1841-1919) arrived by train at Saskatoon, the capital of the Canadian province of Saskatchewan. He had traveled to Saskatoon to lay the foundation of the first university in Saskatchewan. On the platform, he noticed a bright newspaper boy, from whom he bought a newspaper. He asked the newspaper boy how business was going and expressed hope that he would "later make it." After a lively exchange of views, the 15-year-old newspaper boy suddenly said, "Good, Prime Minister, I have to take care of my business now and, unfortunately, I can no longer waste time with you."

47 years later, the newspaper boy John George Diefenbaker actually did become something, namely Canadian Prime Minister, an office he held from 1957-1963. Diefenbaker died in 1979, almost 84 years old. According to his last will, he was to be buried on the campus of Saskatoon University, the foundation of which helped him to meet Prime Minister Lauriel in 1910. His body was brought to Saskatoon in a funeral train and so Diefenbaker returned to the train station, where his career as a newspaper boy began.

The Canadian Pacific train station, built in 1908, was closed to passengers in the 1990s but is a protected building due to its castle-like style. The trains of the Canadian company Via Rail stop today in the sober New Saskatoon Railway Station. There was also a Canadian National Railway (CNR) station in the city. A shopping center was later built on the site. When it was renovated in the 1990s, the facade was changed to resemble that of the old CNR station.

From London to Berlin

Even before the First World War, you could take the train from London to Berlin without changing trains; not in Europe, but rather in Canada. London is a large city in the state of Ontario and Berlin was once the name of another larger city in the same state. Many Germans lived in the former Berlin and there is still a big Oktoberfest in the city today. However, in World War I the name was deemed no longer appropriate and Berlin (and with it its train station) was renamed Kitchener in 1916 after the British field marshal. Anyhow, passenger trains still stop at this city's train station. However, you can no longer travel by train from Berlin to London.

⊙ Pétain and the renaming

The Canadian Pacific Railway (CPR) was less fortunate in naming a station in the Kettle Valley in southern British Columbia. This railway line was a great challenge due to the difficult mountain topography in western Canada, where 5000 workers were temporarily involved in the railway construction. The railway line was completed in 1916. In the same year, during the First World War, the Frenchman Philippe Pétain became the 'hero of Verdun' after succesfully holding the city against the Germans. The railway company decided to name a station Pétain on the new railway line. In 1940, however, Pétain became head of the Vichy government, which collaborated with the Germans and which was located in the unoccupied part of France. As a result, he had changed from a hero to a collaborator. In 1940, the CPR renamed the station Odlum after a Canadian general. This station did not last long either because the snowy winters and the competition from large semi-trucks hit the railway line in such a way that it gradually shut down since the 1960s, and a cycle path was created on its route (in line with the policy `Rails to Trails´).

⊙ Toronto Union Station

Today's Toronto Union Station building was officially opened on August 6, 1927.
The Prince of Wales Edward came on special occasion from Great Britain and ceremoniously cut an opening ribbon with golden scissors.

On the wall of the large counter hall (nicknamed the Great Hall), the names of important destinations that can be reached by train from Toronto have been engraved halfway up. This includes the city of Sault Ste. Marie, which was misspelled as Sault St Marie. To date, the error has not been corrected.

Montreal CPR Windsor Station

The former Windsor station in Montreal is one of the most impressive station buildings in North America.
The Romanesque Revival-style building was designed by New York architect Bruce Price and later a tower was added. It was so large because it served as the headquarters of the Canadian Pacific Railway. When it was completed in 1889, the station building was advertised with the motto `Beats all creation. The new CPR station.´ In 1993, however, the rail connection to the Windsor station was cut and today the complex is purely an office building.

Montreal Gare Centrale / Central Station

The Gare Centrale / Central Station, built in 1943, is now the most important train station in Montreal. Something happened here in 1984 that is unusual for the relatively safe Canada. A bomb exploded in the station, killing 3 French tourists. A retired former American soldier is said to have planted the bomb to protest against Pope John Paul II's visit to Canada.
However, more typical of Canada are attempts to protect against the cold winters. The station, whose tracks run through the tunnel, has a direct connection via the Halles de la Gare to the underground Ville Souterraine/ Underground City - the largest underground complex worldwide with 32 km of pedestrian tunnels connecting shopping centers, apartment buildings, banks, hotels, Museums, universities

and subway stationst - hus avoiding the cold winter temperatures on the surface.

Quebec-Gare du Palais

The Chateau Frontenac is a hotel built by the Canadian Pacific Railway in 1893 and dominates the Québec skyline. Five years earlier, the railway company in Banff had already built a similarly spectacular hotel. Other impressive hotels followed, such as Place Viger (1898) in Montreal (once with a train station) and Royal York (1929) in Toronto. With these representative buildings, one wanted to attract tourists and wealthy passengers. The Gare du Palais de Québec station, built in 1915, is clearly based on the style of the Chateau Frontenac. From 1976 to 1985, no trains stopped here. Today, however, the Gare du Palais is again a VIA rail station.

Winnipeg

The central location of Winnipeg within Canada (the province of Manitoba, whose capital is Winnipeg, also has the nickname 'Keystone Province') meant that several railway companies served the city. When today's Winnipeg Union Station opened in 1911, the Canadian Northern Railroad intended to outperform the nearby Canadian Pacific station with the station building. The architects of the splendid New York Grand Central Terminal were accordingly commissioned to build a splendid reception building. The rotunda with its glass dome is particularly impressive. However, the floor of the entrance hall has cracks. These are said to have been created by in the 1940s soldiers who marched through the building partly in vibration-inducing cadence and with sturdy shoes.

Churchill and the polar bears

Not only in the prairie town of Winnipeg, which is nicknamed 'Winterpeg,' is it quite cold in winter, but also in the whole province, which is also jokingly called 'Manisnowba.' This is especially true for the town of Churchill on Hudson Bay, where even polar bears live. The polar bears have come closer to the city in recent decades, which has spurred tourism and lead to the city's nickname 'Polar Bear Capital of the World.' This also generates passenger traffic for the rail link between Winnipeg and Churchill, and thus 3 passenger trains of the Canadian Via Rail connect the two cities every week (the journey takes 36 hours and uses the tracks of the Hudson Bay Railway in the northern part). The station of the polar bear town of Churchill was only built in 1929 and is now a protected building.

Vancouver Waterfront Station

Until 1979, the waterfront station was the Pacific endpoint of the transcontinental passenger trains of the railroad company CPR. The column-decorated neo-classical building is painted in brown and white colors. Perhaps it is because Starbucks opened the first branch outside of the United States inside this station in 1987.

2. USA ('lower 48 states')

In 1916, the US rail network reached its peak with a length of 409,000 km, of which 150,000 km have since been decommissioned. There was also a dense tram network that connected the suburbs and offered a coherent network from Boston to Philadelphia. There is little left of this network either. Of the 80,000 stations in the United States, around 10,000 remain today, but only about 500 are served by the US passenger company Amtrak. Amtrak was created in the early 1970s by a state initiative to save the remains of the Pennsylvania Railways passenger company and to maintain a minimum level of rail passenger transport, which private rail companies - who were concentrating on more profitable freight transport - were no longer interested.

After the Second World War, rail passenger transport - which was privately operated as in Europe - quickly went downhill as a result of competition from airplanes, cars, and buses. The faster forms of transport drained passenger traffic from the railroad over longer distances as the large-scale of the country, its urban sprawl, and the growth of private car transport reduced the need for local public transport. Only in the Boston-Washington corridor remains a considerable amount of rail passenger traffic, where today there are regular-service trains and high-speed trains. Yet, the quality of operation for these lines is impaired as the rail companies only partially own the tracks. In contrast to passenger transport, rail freight transport has developed well in North America. In no other country is the railroad carrying as many tonne-kilometers as in the USA. This is due to the large transport distances - which suit railways - and to the efficient private freight railroad companies, which are not hindered in their operation (as in Europe) by borders, various track gauges, and power systems.

2.1 New York City and State

New York Grand Central Terminal

Built in 1903, Grand Central Terminal is the largest train station in the world by number of tracks with 44 platforms and 67 tracks on two levels. In terms of the number of passengers (200,000) and station users (750,000) per day, it also ranks first in America. A popular meeting point (`by the golden clock´) is a huge four-sided clock above the information desk. The current value of the clock, which was made from opal, is estimated at over $ 10 million. The ceiling of the entrance hall shows what New Yorkers rarely see in the skyscraper canyons: the stars of the night sky. Of the 2500 stars, 59 are electrically illuminated; originally by 40-watt bulbs and today by LEDs. However, the starry sky is mirror-inverted, which led to embarrassment at the opening as it was explained that the template - a manuscript from the Middle Ages - shows the hypothetical view from the outside of space. There is also a dark ring in the middle of the constellations. In the fifties, in response to the Soviet Sputnik, a rocket was set up in the entrance hall to demonstrate America's technical capabilities. The hole was drilled to adjust the position of the missile. For documentation reasons, the traces of the hole were later not painted over. The Grand Central Terminal celebrated its 100th birthday in early February 2013. In addition to the many books that are available about the station, there is so much to report on, such as, a whispering gallery in front of an oyster bar, secret access for the President, a Tiffany watch, a hidden library and more.

Information desk in the concourse

Grand Central Terminal or Station?

Grand Central is a terminus and is therefore called Terminal and not Station in American English. However, many foreigners, in addition to New Yorkers, say station. In New York, there is even the expression "As busy as Grand Central Station." This is partly due to the previous building, which was originally called the Grand Central Depot but was later named the Grand Central Station. Both names were actually not quite right since the "station" was also a terminal. Under the current station, 5 subway lines stop at their own Grand Central subway station. A link between the station and the Long Island Railroad has been under construction since 2001. It will be completed in 2022 and is expected today to cost over $ 11 billion, making it the most expensive local transportation project in North America. Even then, the terminal paradoxically does not become a station because the Long Island Railroad trains are to enter a new 15-story underground terminal that will have 8 tracks. This will make the Grand Central complex even busier and more interesting, but it will still remain a terminal.

Facade (with Tiffany-clock) and urban context of GCT

Grand Central and the Foamer

Die-hard railroad freaks, which are also called bumper-kissers in Germany, are nicknamed Foamer in the United States because they are said to foam with enthusiasm when they see a train. You will hardly find foamers in the Grand Central Terminal. While this station is delightful as an architectural icon steeped in history and important for New York fans, it is not very interesting for locomotive fans. Grand Central is now a purely local transport station, and only three local transport routes to the north are served by this station. Standardized subway-like commuter cars without locomotives depart from rather shabby platforms. That was not always so. From 1902 to 1967, Grand Central was the starting point for 20th Century Limited, a luxurious long-distance train to Chicago. Before each departure, a red carpet was rolled out on the platform for the passengers.

Grand Central's rescue

The much-regretted demolition of Pennsylvania Station (as shown below) has helped to protect Grand Central from a similar fate, yet, there were other reasons why Grand Central was redeveloped rather than demolished. At first, the future of the station did not look so good. The New York Central Terminal, the Pennsylvania Station, and later the Pennsylvania Railroad - to which the station belonged - urgently needed money because of declining income from passenger transport due to their ever-increasing competition from airplanes and cars. Additionally, Midtown Manhattan is a sought-after office location, as not far from Grand Central are the Chrysler Building and the United Nations skyscraper. As early as 1954, proposals were made to demolish Grand Central and replace it with a skyscraper that was to be taller than the Empire State Building. Even when the New York City Landmark Preservation Commission granted New York City Landmark status to Grand Central in 1967 (even National Historic Landmark status in 1976), the station building was still not entirely saved. The monument protection commission rejected the gigantic skyscraper plans in 1968, but in 1969, the railway company proposed a 59-story skyscraper that would only have demolished the outer walls but would have left the station's walk-in hall intact. The Monument Protection Commission also rejected this proposal. In response, the railway company sued and won, but the city appealed the verdict. Finally, in 1978, the Supreme Court confirmed the station's landmark status. In 1991, the Amtrak long-distance transport company withdrew completely from the station because a new connection made it possible for all long-distance trains to travel directly to Penn Station. The New York public transport company MTA took over the station in 1994, and since then it has had no plans to tear it down.

New York Penn (Pennsylvania) station

New York once had a second magnificent station building: Pennsylvania (Penn) Station, built in 1910. The inside was modeled on the Caracalla thermal baths and the outside portals were modeled on the Brandenburg Gate in Berlin. However, the existing air rights above this station were too valuable not to be used more intensively. If the architect McKim had planned an office tower in the railway complex, the ensemble could have survived commercially. However, the station building was demolished in the mid-1960s against unsuccessful protests by architectural critics, such as Canadian Jane Jacobs (1916-2006), in order to build the Madison Square Garden complex in its place. But the hasty demolition was felt by the New Yorkers as a loss. Photos of the broken caryatids that ended up in a rubble site made people feel guilty. And one writer complained that one used to drive into the city like a king, but now (with the underground train station) sneaked into the city like a rat. The preservation of historical monuments in New York was eventually strengthened, and the equally magnificent Central Station was spared a similar fate.

The old Pennsylvania Station

World Trade Center Station

One of the most interesting train stations in New York was the Hudson Terminal, above which two 22-story skyscrapers towered. With the construction of the World Trade Center and the opening of the World Trade Center PATH station, the station was closed.

In 1993, a bomb attack was carried out on the World Trade Center, which also caused part of the ceiling of the PATH train station to collapse. Several passengers were trapped in the station. On September 11th, 2001, the station was closed shortly after the first plane hit the north tower of the World Trade Center. At 9:10 a.m., the train company sent another train to evacuate rail workers plus a homeless person from the station.

The PATH station was also destroyed by the attack. Two years later, a provisional station was opened in November 2003. A new, spectacular station designed by the Spanish architect Calatravahas has since opened.

⊙ Rockefeller and the train accident in Angola

On December 18, 1867, the young John D. Rockefeller, who would later become a billionaire, left his humble home in Cleveland to take a business trip to New York by train. He said goodbye to his wife Laura and his one-year-old daughter and hurried to the station to catch the 6:40 train to Buffalo, where he wanted to board a train to New York. He had already sent his luggage ahead of him, but Rockefeller arrived in Cleveland's Union Station a few minutes late. The already loaded luggage left without him. The train chugged along Lake Erie and had almost reached Buffalo when in Angola (which was given this name by African missionaries) the two rear carriages jumped out of the tracks and plunged down a ravine. Both wagons went up in flames. 50 passengers burned to the point of being unrecognizable and others were seriously injured. Rockefeller, who reached the station late, would have been sitting in one of the rear carriages. He instead took a later train, which was forced to stop in Angola because of the accident. Rockefeller became aware of the catastrophe he had escaped and telegraphed his wife from the train station to say that he was alive because he had just missed the accident.

⊙ Theodore Roosevelt and the message

Theodore Roosevelt (1858-1919), also known as Teddy (and hence the namesake of the teddy bear), was considered a nature and hiking enthusiast and opponent of automobiles. In September 1901, Roosevelt, who had been Vice President of the United States since the beginning of the year, was on a hiking trip with his family in the Adirondack Mountains in northern New York. In the mountains, a runner told him that President McKinley had been assassinated in an exhibition in Buffalo and was dying. A hasty carriage brought Roosevelt to the North Creek station.

Roosevelt was given a telegram that said McKinley had died at 2:30 a.m. Today there is a museum in the wooden station building, which commemorates the events of the time.

Buffalo and the buffalo

The Art Deco-style, tower-like Buffalo Central Terminal, built in 1929, is one of the most architecturally important station buildings in the United States. However, in 1979, it lost its function as a train station and as a result increasingly decayed. In 1997, the station building was therefore sold to a local renovation association for $1. Only a partial renovation has been completed since then, but at the least various events have already taken place in the station, including weddings and an Oktoberfest.

☞: Because of the city's name, once a stuffed bison was on display in the station's walk-in hall. The stuffed animal, which belonged to the local science museum, was supposed to advertise for the museum. But due to passengers passing by and rubbing its hands, the bison's fur was soon so worn that it had to be replaced with a plaster model. This plaster model was later destroyed by negligence. Finally, a sculpture called Progress was placed on the station square. When it was prepared to be transported to a sculpture park, the sculpture was also badly damaged.

Buffalo Central Terminal (Photo: Wikipedia)

⊙ Elmira and Mark Twain

Elmira is a medium-sized town (approximately 30,000 inhabitants) in western New York, not far from the Pennsylvania border. The city was originally called Newtown. When the city council met in 1808 to discuss a more original name for the city, a mother is said to have called out loudly for her daughter "Elmira, Elmira," and so a new name had been found.

In 1849, the city got a train station. The city was nicknamed Hellmira because a camp for captive southern soldiers was established in the American Civil War. On a trip to Egypt and the Holy Land, the American writer Samuel Langhorne Clemens, known worldwide under his pen-name Mark Twain, met Charles J. Langdon from Elmira. Langdon invited Twain to Elmira, where he fell in love with his sister Olivia Langdon, whom he married in Elmira in 1870.

Twain's sister-in-law owned a farm on the outskirts of Elmira and this was where the Twains were to spend their summers for the next 20 years (Twain had his main residence in Hartford / Connecticut). In a garden shed on the property, Twain wrote some of his most important works, including The Adventures of Huckleberry Finn.

A chicken farm also belonged to the property. There is an anecdote about this, which, however, does not seem particularly credible. Twain had commissioned a chicken coop to arrive by train. He sent a servant to transport the chicken coop from the station to the farm with a horse-drawn carriage, but he came back with something bigger than a chicken coop: he had loaded the wooden station building.

Richardsonian Romanesque

The American architect Henry Hobson Richardson (1838-1886) coined a style in American architecture in the 19th century, called Richardsonian Romanesque. The architecture in the Boston area was particularly influenced by this style. Several train stations, especially in the northeastern United States, were built in this style in the 19th century. Richardson himself, who died at the age of 47, designed the following Boston & Albany Railroad stations in Massachusetts: Palmer, North Easton, Framingham, Holyoke, Newton, Wellesley Hills, and Union Station in New London, Connecticut. Several other train stations in the USA have been influenced in their architecture by Richardson's style. At the end of the 19th century, by the way, the neo-Romanesque architectural style with its simple, massive forms was considered particularly German and the favorite style of the German emperor. After the annexation of Lorraine, the Metz train station was built in this style.

Portland, Maine and the seagull

In 1961, a wrecking ball brought down the beautiful neo-Gothic tower of the Union Station building in Portland, Maine. As the last station user, a seagull flew quickly out of the tower. Similarly to Penn Station in New York, the rash demolition of the reception building, in the place of which a shopping mall was built, caused a rethinking and strengthening of monument protection in Portland.

Worcester Union Stations Rebirth

With the decline of rail passenger transport since the 1960s, several stations were abandoned. Due to the decline in passenger numbers and the merger of railway companies, many Union Stations were no longer needed operationally. After initial decay of many buildings, stations in central locations of large cities soon found other uses, such as shopping centers and hotels. However, some stations in small towns were also successfully revitalized, and new uses often only emerged after a previous renovation, for example, by a regional development company.

The Union Station of Worcester in Massachusetts was abandoned in 1975 and fell into disrepair for two decades. In 1995, it was purchased and redeveloped by the Worcester Development Authority. No expense was spared, as even the two imposing clock towers, which had long since been demolished, were rebuilt. The renovated station building is now one of the most beautiful in America and can be rented for private parties.

Worcester Union Station

Mount Washington and the rack railway

The mountain station of the rack railway on the 1917 m. high Mount Washington in the state of New Hampshire is the highest railway station in the eastern US. Surprisingly, the rack railway, opened in 1869, is also the oldest mountain-climbing railway in the world. The Rigibahn, the first mountain rack railway in the cogwheel country of Switzerland - built according to the cogwheel drive principle invented in 1863 by the Swiss Nikolaus Riggenbach - was opened only 2 years later. Ulysses S. Grant and Albert Einstein, among others, traveled to Mount Washington by rack railway. In 1994, Marshfield Station was opened as a new valley station in the old architectural style but with modern service facilities.

Bretton Woods

At the foot of Mount Washington is the Bretton Woods Hotel. It was here that the famous Bretton Woods Currency Conference was held in 1944, with participants traveling by special trains to nearby Bretton Woods Station. The station is now closed to rail traffic and houses the Fabyan's Station restaurant.

Providence

When the first Union Station of Providence - located on the New York-Boston railway line in the capital of Rhode Island - was opened in 1847, the station building was the longest in the USA.

In 1898, this station was replaced by a new building. However, the tracks leading to the station close to downtown were considered a "Chinese wall" that hindered urban development. Therefore, the railway lines were moved to the outside, and offices and a restaurant moved into the old station building. In 1986, Providence got a new train station, whose simple clock tower somewhat resembles the one in Stuttgart. Its glass roof, in the form of an inverted saucer, is somewhat reminiscent of a mosque. With over 600,000 passengers in 2011, it is one of the top 20 US stations of Amtrak.

Cannondale and the bicycle manufacturer

From Grand Central Terminal, the *Metro-North Line* runs to Cannondale, Connecticut. In the 1970s, an employee of a small bicycle company called the phone company from the public phone at this station to apply for a company connection. When he was asked for the name of the still-unnamed company, he hesitated and said, "Hm,...Cannondale." This is how the well-known bicycle manufacturer came to his name.

White River Junction and the weather vane

In the book *The Railroad in the USA*, Joe Welsh shows a picture taken in 1974 of the station tower of White River Junction in Vermont. The tower has windows all around, and on its roof is a weather vane in the shape of a steam locomotive. But in later years, the author writes, there was nothing left of the lovingly crafted locomotive weather vane. It became the victim of weathervane collectors.

Boston South

Boston's South Station was the station with the highest passenger numbers in the world when it opened in 1899. In 1913, South Station still had more passengers than New York Grand Central Terminal with 100,000 passengers per day. The platform hall, which consisted of a single wide arch, was considered one of the largest in the world but was demolished in 1930 due to corrosion by the salty sea air. When GIs were streaming back from Europe in 1945, passenger records were set once again, with 135,000 passengers per day. Passenger numbers declined after World War II, but Amtrak's well-developed commuter rail system and connection to the Boston-Washington major route continue to provide (by American standards) high passenger numbers of over 30,000 per day.

Boston South Station

Boston North

North of Boston, long-distance rail traffic is thinning out noticeably. Due to this development, Boston North station has less than a third of the passenger numbers of Boston South. However, traffic is increasing again, and more than 1000 passengers a day are boarding long-distance trains and 10,000 local trains at Boston North.

2.3 Rest of the North East

⊙ The train station of Gettysburg

The Battle of Gettysburg in Pennsylvania won by the Northern Army and in which 46,000 soldiers died, played an important role in the American Civil War. During the battle, the town's train station - which was built in 1859 - served as a military hospital, and many of the soldiers left it afterward. On November 18, 1863, American President Abraham Lincoln arrived here to give a landmark speech the following day at Gettysburg War Cemetery. Today, the station is called Lincoln Station, and because of the historical importance of the place, it was renovated a few years ago and can be visited.

⊙ Jersey City and Lincoln's Savior

In 1864, Robert Lincoln, the son of Abraham Lincoln, changed trains at the Jersey City train station on his way from Harvard to Washington. Due to the crowd on the platform, he, unfortunately, fell into the gap between the train and the platform, Luckily, a man pulled him back up and saved his life. It was Edward Booth, whose younger brother John Wilkes Booth shot Robert's father, US President Abraham Lincoln (1809-1865), a year later.

Baltimore Mount Clare Station

Baltimore had the first railway line, and with Mount Clare Station, built in 1829, the first railway station in the USA. The Mount Clare complex also included the first railway vehicle factory in the USA. Therefore Mount Clare is considered *"the birthplace of American railroading."*
Unfortunately, there is nothing left of the old station building. Yet, a second station building from the year 1851

is still standing. Additionally, the round railway shed, which today houses the B&O Railroad Museum, is also 125 years old. Unfortunately, the roof of the museum collapsed in February 2003 due to the heavy snow load, whereby also some exhibition pieces were damaged. However, this railway museum is still one of the most important in the world.

Baltimore Camden Station

Camden Station in Baltimore is one of the oldest continuously used station buildings in the world. The station building with its classic Italian style was built as early as 1857, and it did not lose its station function until the 1980s. Today, it houses the sports museum *Sports Legends* at Camden Yards. In its renovated state, with its tall, slender central tower and two side towers, it is one of the most beautiful former station buildings on the east coast. In the railway sense, however, the station function of the complex was not completely lost, as trains still stop at the platforms.

Baltimore Pennsylvania Station and the statue

In 2004, the city's art-in-architecture funds were used to erect a 15-meter-high aluminum statue called *Male/Female* in front of Baltimore's Pennsylvania Station, which has since been controversial. Critics say that the huge statue, which stands close to the façade, distracts from the station's beaux-arts architecture, and the local newspaper *The Baltimore Sun* has been writing against the statue ever since. One journalist said the statue looked like the robot Gort in the film *The Day the Earth Stood Still*.

☉ Westinghouse and the test near Pittsburgh

One day, the American inventor George Westinghouse (1846-1914) was on his way by train to a business appointment in the city of Troy. Suddenly, the train stopped abruptly, and Westinghouse was yanked out of his seat. He looked out the window and saw why the train had to stop: two freight trains had collided. He asked the injured brakeman of the wrecked train how something like that could happen in broad daylight when you could see and brake the oncoming train from far away. He said, that one could brake, but the brakes would not work fast enough. This got Westinghouse thinking, and he developed an air pressure brake based on existing technology. When Westinghouse asked the president of the *New York Central Railroad*, Cornelius Vanderbilt, for support for the invention, he sent back his letter with the remark, "I have no time to waste on fools."

In order to convince the railways, the invention had to be tested in operation, but many railway companies refused. Finally, the *Panhandle Railroad* was willing to give it a try on the Pittsburgh-Steubenville line in April 1869. When the air-braked train came out of a tunnel near Pittsburgh, Westinghouse and his engineer saw a horse and cart come to a stop on a level crossing ahead. With whiplashes, the coachman tried to drive the horses on, but they bucked, and the coachman fell on the rails. Westinghouse quickly opened the valve of the air brake, and the train came to a halt a few meters in front of the carriage. After this test, the air brake became widely accepted, and Westinghouse formed the *Westinghouse Air Brake Company*. Now, he received a letter from the railway tycoon Vanderbilt. The answer from Westinghouse, "I have no time to waste on fools."

Pittsburgh - the underrated city

Pittsburgh was once the leading American steel city and was considered "hell with the lid taken off" because of the environmental pollution caused by industry.

But connoisseurs also see Pittsburgh as one of the most attractive US cities. Pittsburgh is located at the confluence of three rivers has many bridges, an interesting skyline, and is set in a beautiful landscape. Furthermore, important universities are located in the city. No wonder that the city's most important train station, the Pittsburgh Union Station, also known as Penn Station, is not in a state of industrial decline. The multi-story station building, designed by Washington Union Station architect Daniel Burnham, houses today's luxury apartments, and the entrance hall serves as the entrance hall to the residential tower. Despite the residential use of the station building, trains still stop at the station.

⊙ Princeton Junction and Albert Einstein

Albert Einstein (1879-1955) had been awarded the Nobel Prize for Physics in 1921. He was working in Berlin at the time, but his scientific success earned him numerous honorary doctorates, including one from Princeton University (New Jersey) on the American East Coast. He traveled there in December 1932, but did not return to Germany in 1933 due to the Nazi takeover, and spent the rest of his life in this university town. It is said that Einstein enjoyed sitting at Princeton Junction station and watching the trains go by.

⊙ Frank Sinatra and Ramsey Station

The US entertainer Frank Sinatra (1915-1998) was born in Hoboken, New Jersey, and was the son of Italian immigrants. In 1948, after achieving fame, he moved to

Palm Springs, California. Yet, he somehow seemed to miss the railroad, which was abundant in his native state. In a house on his estate, he built a huge model railway layout and a building that was a copy of the Ramsey railway station in New Jersey.

Philadelphia Graver's Lane

In the book *1001 Buildings You Must See Before You Die*, the small Graver's Lane Station in Philadelphia, built in 1882 by Frank Furness, is the only American station of the 9 stations listed. The author liked the fact that all parts of the building look as if they should be much bigger, which gives the station an interesting, playful appearance. The architect Albert Kesley wrote, "The whole sweep of the structure there, relatively unimportant as it is, is masterful."

⊙ Philadelphia 30th Street Station

When Philadelphia's 30th Street Station opened in 1930, it was packed with innovations. Its flat roof had been designed so that small planes could land on it. The station also had a pneumatic tube system and an internal electronic communication system. On September 13, 2001, there was something special again. On that day, the US writer and satirist Neal Pollack (b. 1970) gave a reading in the men's room at the station.

Benjamin Franklin was born in Philadelphia in 1706, and efforts were made to rename 30th Street Station - the city's most important train station - *Ben Franklin Station* to mark his 300th birthday in 2006.

30th Street Station (Ausgang zur Stadt)

Yet, because of fears that a station could be confused with existing Penn Stations, everything remained the same.

30th Street Station (Station concourse)

Scranton Lackawanna

In the 19th century, the town of Scranton in Pennsylvania developed into an industrial town that supplied the whole of America with railway tracks due to the local deposits of high-quality anthracite coal. The first electric tram in the USA ran in Scranton in 1886, which is why the city was given the nickname "electric city."

However, after a natural disaster in 1959, when the Susquehanna River flooded the mines, mining came to an end. Since the 1970s, the textile industry also migrated, and Scranton became a shrinking city of the industrial Rust Belt. At least a solution was found for Scranton's neo-classical Lackawanna Station, built in 1907-1908, which became a hotel in 1983. After renovation in 2006, the building, lined with Siena marble and hand-painted tiles, is now a three-star hotel in the Radisson chain.

Hoboken Terminal

The Hoboken Terminal in New Jersey is an intermodal transportation hub where intercity rail, bus, light rail, and ferry lines connect Hoboken with New York on the other side of the Hudson. The entrance hall, with its Tiffany glass tiles, is considered one of the most beautiful in North America. The 69-meter-high clock tower, which was demolished in the early 1950s, was rebuilt to celebrate the station's 100th anniversary. Several new features were first tried out in this station. The first scheduled electric train in North America departed here, and for the first time, a central air conditioning system was installed in a public building. The platform roofs developed by the American engineer Lincoln Bush in 1906, with their central slot for steam extraction, which made large platform hall roofs superfluous, were also first installed in Hoboken.

2.4 Washington

⊙ Washington Baltimore and Potomac Station

On July 2, 1881, two months after his inauguration as the 20th American president, James Abram Garfield was assassinated at Washington's Baltimore and Potomac Station. When Garfield boarded the train to Williamstown, MA, he was hit by two bullets fired by Charles J. Guiteau, who was disappointed that he had not been granted a position as U.S. ambassador to France. But the bullets, one of which penetrated the body, were not fatal. However, the president was doomed by the fact that several doctors were drilling around in the wound with unsterilized fingers to find the bullet. Finally, inventor Alexander Graham Bell tried a metal detector. He concluded that the bullet must be deep inside the body. The doctors cut open the president without finding the bullet. Bell's metal detector had not located the bullet, but a metal spring in the president's bed. The doctors' botched job finally killed the president 80 days after the assassination.

With the opening of Washington's Union Station, the assassination station was closed in 1907 and later demolished.

Washington Union Station

Opened in 1907, Union Station in Washington was once considered the largest station in America, if not the world. The station concourse was considered the world's largest space under one roof. It had its own presidential suite because, in 1881, the US President James Garfield was shot while waiting for the train in the previous station on Capitol Hill. The neoclassical style of the building incorporates many formal elements of Roman antiquity: the entrance portal imitates the Arch of Constantine in Rome, the hall is reminiscent of an oversized Roman basilica, and the façade contains 36 statues of Roman legionaries. The later built central station of Milan was inspired by the architecture of Union Station. There are also several architectural similarities with the old Pennsylvania Station in New York. Similar to the old Pennsylvania Station, the Pennsylvania Railroad wanted to demolish Union Station in the 1960s, and build other things on the property. Luckily, Congress intervened, and the building was saved. In the seventies, however, it fell into disrepair, and in 1981, the station was closed. Yet, after a renovation and expansion into a shopping center, it was reopened in 1988. Today, more than 50,000 people use the station every day, including 13,000 long-distance passengers.

Union Station and the train without brakes

On the morning of January 1, 1953, the brakes failed on a Federal Express train 3 km before Union Station in Washington on sloping terrain. The driver warned the station by radio, and the station concourse was cleared as the train was speeding towards the station. The locomotive hit the buffer stop at about 40 km/h, jumped off the tracks, destroyed a platform attendant's cabin, took out a newspaper stand, and was about to break through the wall into the station concourse. However, the weight of the locomotive caused the ceiling of the platform to give way, and the train crashed into the basement of the station. Luckily, no one was killed, and the passengers in the rear compartments believed that it was just a slightly more abrupt train braking. The basement, where the locomotive came to a halt, is now the station's catering level.

2.5 Michigan

☉ Port Huron and Thomas Alva Edison

The American inventor Thomas Alva Edison (1847-1931) was born in Milan, Ohio. But, since the town did not have a railway connection, the family moved to Port Huron in Michigan when he was seven years old. The rail connection from there to Detroit was to play an important role in Edison's early entrepreneurial activities. He was already earning his money as a paperboy on the trains at the age of 11. A few years later, he even published his own newspaper, which he produced on a printing press on the train station and sold to passengers. Once, as he was running after the train, the conductor pulled him into the carriage by his ears, causing a tear in his inner ear, presumably a reason for Edison's later hearing loss.

Edison once saw three-year-old Jimmie MacKenzie playing on the tracks as a train approached. Edison saved his life, and his father, a station employee, was so grateful that he taught Edison to how to use the telegraph, which helped him get a telegraph job, and spurred his further development as an inventor.

Holland in Michigan

The city of Holland in Michigan got its name because it was founded by Dutchmen in the 1840s. For more than 100 years, the population was over 90 percent of Dutch descent. It was not until after the Second World War that an ethnic mix was established. In the city stands the last original Dutch windmill, which left the Netherlands with official permission. There is also a canal, a wooden shoe factory, and brick houses. Only the railway station with its modern functional architecture is not reminiscent of Holland if it weren't for the many tulips in the flowerbeds and green spaces that reach down to the tracks.

⊙ Ann Arbor and the mixed-up suitcase

The neo-Gothic styled Michigan Central Railway Depot of the town of Ann Arbor, not far from Detroit, was considered "the finest station on the line from Buffalo to Chicago," after its construction in 1886. In 1970, the station building was sold to Chuck Muer, who restored it and established the Gandy Dancer restaurant inside. Gandy Dancer was once a nickname for the track workers. In its 84-year history, the station had seen many US presidents who stopped here by train on their campaign trail, including Roosevelt, Nixon, and Kennedy. William Howard Taft's campaign train also stopped in Ann Arbor.

Taft was the 27th President of the United States from 1909-1913. With a weight of over 140 kg, he was so heavy that a special bathtub had to be purchased for him at the White House because he got stuck in the original tub. In November 1915, long out of office, Taft visited the University of Michigan in Ann Arbor to give a speech. In the university guest house, however, he discovered that his luggage had been mixed up at the train station because his suitcase contained only women's clothes. Taft was less concerned about himself than about the unfortunate woman, who probably didn't know what to do with his tent-like clothes. Finally, the speech was postponed until the former president's replacement clothes were obtained.

Chelsea and the iron cable

Chelsea, located west of Ann Arbor on the Michigan Central Line, has a small wooden train station. Its predecessor, built in 1850, was the city's first commercial building, but it was actually just a modest hut, as Chelsea was only a small village at that time. Yet, with the railway came growth, and in the 1870s, the citizens of the town wanted a more prestigious station building. The railway company, however, remained inactive. So, one night, young men fastened an iron cable to the station. The other end, they attached to an incoming train. When the train departed, it pulled the station with it, and its wooden parts were scattered along the railway line. The Michigan Central Company finally had to build a new station in Chelsea in 1880. It is still there today, but trains have not stopped here since 1981.

Detroit Michigan Central Station

The American car city of Detroit is considered the epitome of industrial decay. Once one of the richest cities in the USA, the "motor city" has lost more than half its inhabitants since 1950, when it was the fifth-largest city in the USA with 1.8 million inhabitants. The white middle class, in particular, has migrated to the suburbs. Despite attempts to breathe life into the inner city, the city center is characterized by modern ruins. This is also true of the city's main train station, Michigan Central Station, an eighteen-story monumental building that now stands abandoned in the city's wasteland. This station was opened in 1913 after another station burned down. The entrance hall was modeled after a Roman bath and had marble walls. The railway station is located just outside the city. At the time, it was hoped that the development of the city would follow the station. Yet, the boom in car production under Henry Ford was followed by the economic crisis of the twenties. After World War II, rail traffic declined further, and attempts were made to sell the building, but no interested parties were found. In 1967, the entrance hall and other facilities were closed. In the seventies, the newly founded company Amtrak took over rail passenger transport. Yet, already in 1988, the last train left the station, and the station was later sold for less than $80,000. However, all plans to re-utilize the station have failed so far.

⊙ Battle Creek and the Cornflakes

The city of Battle Creek in southern Michigan is called *Cereal City* because this is where cornflakes were invented and where the Kellogg Group still has its headquarters. The physician John Harvey Kellogg (1852-1943) ran a sanatorium in Battle Creek, which he managed according to holistic principles, whereby a vegetarian diet played an important role. In 1894, Harvey developed what was later known as *Corn Flakes*. His more enterprising brother Will Keith Kellogg (1860-1951) then founded the *Battle Creek Toasted Corn Flake Company* in February 1906, which has been known as the *Kellogg Company* since 1922. It is now the largest grain processor in the world. Also, in 1906, the two-towered Grand Trunk Depot station was opened in Battle Creek. The local newspaper saw the station in 1907 as "one of the most elaborate and finely finished depots in the country." However, the station also shows a strange mixture of styles. The ground floor is made of grey granite walls with brick façade on top with baroque gables and Spanish style towers. The luxurious waiting area was lined with marble and had a barrel roof with gilded Renaissance-style ceiling decorations. The station was closed in 1971 but served as an office for the railway company until 1988. Today, it is home to the South Michigan Community Action Agency, which received funding from the W.K. Kellogg Foundation to purchase and renovate the building.

Niles and the light show

The city of Niles in Michigan has a sandstone station built in 1892, which is still served by Amtrak trains (although only 18,000 people a year board here, so only about 50 a day). The well-preserved, photogenic station building has already attracted several film crews. Scenes of *Continental Divide* with John Belushi and *Midnight Run* with Robert de Niro were shot here. In 1990, a scene for the film *Only the Lonely* was shot here. For this purpose, the station building was decorated with bands of lights. After the shooting was finished, the film crew offered to the light ribbons to the station owner Amtrak for free. But Amtrak cordially declined. Finally, the *Niles Four Flags Garden Club* accepted the light ribbons and decorated the station again in time for Christmas 1991. Since then, on the first weekend in December after nightfall, the lights on the Niles station façade have been turned on, and a small party is held to celebrate.

East Lansing Station and the University

Several American railway station buildings have been converted into restaurants after being closed, for example, in Lansing (Michigan). When the Chicago-Toronto international rail service was resumed, the Amtrak railroad company in Lansing was missing a station building. Finally, Michigan State University in nearby East Lansing, one of the largest universities in America with more than 40,000 students, helped the railway company by providing it with a storage building on the tracks. This way, both Amtrak and the university gained a station.

2.6 Chicago and Illinois

Chicago LaSalle Street Station

There have already been several station buildings at the LaSalle Street location in Chicago.
The first one was built in 1852 but was replaced by a new building as early as 1866, which was destroyed by the great city fire of 1871 but was later rebuilt. The third station was built in 1903 and stood until 1981. In 1959, Hitchcock's thriller *North by Northwest* was filmed here, and in 1973, scenes from the film *The Sting* with Paul Newman and Robert Redford were shot.

Chicago North Western Station

Chicago was once the stronghold of the Hobos because of its central location in the US railway network. The late 19th and early 20th century were the heyday of the Hobos, American migrant workers who used freight trains to travel freely across the country. In Chicago, West Madison Street was considered the "Hobo Capital of the World." It was a concentration of employment agencies that arranged jobs for all parts of the US. The North Western Terminal, located on West Madison Street, was part of the station.
The 1911 Chicago and North Western Terminal station building was demolished in 1984 to make way for the Citicorp Center high-rise, whose lower floors now house the train station. The station is now officially called the *Richard B. Ogilvie Transportation Center* and was named after a Governor of Illinois, who was a strong supporter of the railroad

Chicago Union Station

The waiting area of Chicago's Union Station, built in 1925, is considered one of the most magnificent public covered spaces in the USA. Its nickname is the "Great Hall," and a special feature is its long solid wooden benches. The waiting area and the lobby are similar to that of the old Pennsylvania Station in New York, which was demolished in the early 1960s. While the waiting area survived, the Union Station lobby was destroyed in the 1960s. Chicago's Union Station was also featuring in several movies. In the film *The Untouchables*, a baby stroller slips and rattles down the station stairs to LaSalle Street. Union Station is also the starting point of the long-distance train to Texas.

Chicago Union Station (Bild: Krzysztof Makara)

☉ Ravinia and the orchestra

Highland Park is a wealthy suburb in the northern part of Chicago. Highland Park includes the former Ravinia District artists colony. The *Chicago and Milwaukee Electric Railroad* established the Ravinia Amusement Park here in 1904 to draw in more passengers on the railroad. When the railroad company went bankrupt, Chicago businessmen bought the park and established an annual music festival there. Today, the Ravinia Festival is the oldest outdoor music festival in the USA and is recognized for the high standard of its performances. Louis Armstrong, Duke Ellington, Frank Zappa, Janis Joplin, and Leonard Bernstein, among others, have performed here. The Chicago Symphony Orchestra also moves its performances to the Ravinia grounds during the summer months. However, the concert hall is built very close to the tracks. James Petrillo, the president of the *American Orchestral Musicians Association*, once had the trains stopped when the famous master violinist Jascha Heifetz played. However, the conductor Thomas Beecham, who conducted the Chicago Symphony Orchestra in summer 1940, could not prevail with such wishes. He said that Ravinia was "the only railway station with a resident orchestra," and never performed there again. By the way, Ravinia Park station has only platforms, but no station building. Trains only stop here during the summer concert season.

☉ Pullman 111th Street Station

Pullman 111th Street Station is a relatively sober stop on a Chicago commuter rail line.

The station is named after the American inventor George Mortimer Pullman (1831-1897). Pullman is best known among railroaders for the sleeping car he invented in 1864 (in southern Europe, even long-distance coaches are called

Pullman), which was inspired by riverboats. His commercial breakthrough came in 1865, when Lincoln's body was transported from Washington to Springfield, Illinois in a sleeping car. In 1880, Pullman purchased a 16 km^2 site 20 km south of downtown Chicago to build a manufacturing plant and factory complex.

The architect Spencer Beman is said to have been so proud of his work that he asked Pullman if the settlement could be named after him. To which Pullman replied, "Sure, we'd best take the first half of my last name and the second half of yours." The factory settlement was considered a model town and was called the "world's most perfect town." But Pullman ruled here autocratically and even controlled whether the workers kept their apartments clean enough.

In 1893, there was an economic crisis in the USA, and the demand for sleeping cars declined. Pullman had to lay off workers and cut wages. Yet, the rents in his settlement were not reduced. This triggered a strike of the workers (Pullman Strike). The strike was finally put down with the help of federal troops. Pullman was from now on so unpopular with the trade unions that when he died in 1897, he was buried at night, and several tons of cement were poured into the grave to prevent trade unionists from taking the body out of the grave out of anger and desecrating it.

⊙ Springfield Union Station

Springfield, the capital of the US state of Illinois, was the adopted home of Kentucky-born US President Abraham Lincoln. After Lincoln's death, his body was brought to Springfield on a special train that stopped in many cities. The Springfield Union Station, opened in 1898, saw the last passenger train in 1971 and now serves as Abraham Lincoln Presidential Library.The striking clock tower of the station, which was demolished in 1946, was rebuilt in 2006 and today carries a mast on which the stars and stripes fly.

The eerie station of Decatur

Decatur is a centrally located city in Illinois that has had a railroad link since 1854, and where many trains that ran from Chicago to St. Louis once stopped. Decatur had two stations across the street, Wabash Station and Illinois Central Station. Yet, as passenger traffic declined, Illinois Central Station was demolished in 1951. Wabash Station, which now houses an antique shop, once seemed haunted. As late as the 1940s, railroad employees thought they saw a young woman in white sitting on a bench during the night shift, who disappeared suddenly as they came in. This woman is said to have been married to a man who had to go to war in 1918. A few months later, she received a letter informing her that he would soon be coming home. Full of anticipation, she went to the station on the day of his planned arrival to wait for him. She waited all afternoon to see which passengers got off the trains, but her husband was not among them. Disappointed, she went home and consoled herself by saying that the date had probably been mixed up. But there was no trace of him the next day either. She went to the station every day for a week, but without success. Then she received a telegram from New York. It said that her husband had died in a bus accident in New York while he was on his way to the station and to the train that was to take him home. When she read this, she overdosed on pills in her grief and ended her life. Years later, the young woman dressed in white was still waiting to be seen at the station. However, this haunting has disappeared since the station was closed.

Decatur and haunting number two

Some people think they see a mysterious light from time to time moving along the freight tracks behind Wabash station. The explanation is as follows: Brakemen once traveled on freight trains and used a signal lamp to inform the driver of any problems. Once a freight train stopped at the station, the brakeman got out of his car to inspect the train. He was looking into the gap between two freight cars when the train suddenly started to move. His head was clamped, and he was decapitated. His ghost still walks along the tracks with the lamp. Others believe that it is the ghost of policeman Davenport, who, lamp in hand, caught two criminals in the track area of the station. They fired at him, fled, and Davenport bled to death on the tracks.

Deerfield - No kissing

Deerfield is a commuter railroad station of the Chicago Metra-Suburban rail system. Deerfield hit the headlines in 1979 when the local government established a no-kissing zone at the station. With the rise in gasoline prices after the oil crisis, more and more employees commuted to Chicago by train. Mostly it was men who were brought to the station by their wives by car (so-called 'kiss and ride'). However, the goodbye kisses slowed down traffic, hence the ban. The no kissing signs of the station caused a lot of media interest at that time.

2.7 Other Great Lakes States

Indianapolis Union Station

Unlike in Europe, there was no wave of nationalization of private railway companies in the US at the end of the 19th century. As a result, larger cities began to have more stations operated by different companies. This was extremely cumbersome for people changing trains, so the planners sought to establish centrally located Union Stations to be served by all railway companies. Only New York did not get a Union Station, as the city itself was the final destination of many journeys, and therefore there were few people changing trains, the stations were connected by subway, and the through traffic passed the city on the west side. The first Union Station was already opened in Indianapolis in 1853.

Cincinnati Union Terminal

Cincinnati is located on the Ohio River. Neighborhoods close to the water were repeatedly threatened by its flooding. When looking for a location for the Central Station, flood safety was an important factor. When a site was identified two miles from downtown, the site was raised by 5 meters to provide flood protection. The 500,000 cubic meters of soil required for this was taken from a nearby hill, the Bald Knob, where the results of this soil extraction can still be seen today. The Cincinnati Union Terminal, an Art Deco hemispherical reception building, was finally opened in 1933. Its abbreviation is CUT, which indeed a hill was cut for its construction. Flood safety was achieved, but this could not be said of the local airport Lunken. It was flooded in the great flood of 1937 and was nicknamed Sunken Lunken. Later it was moved to another location.

Cincinnati Union Terminal (Bild: Wikipedia)

Union Station Gary, Indiana

Along with Detroit, Gary, Indiana, is the epitome of a city in decline in the Rust Belt, with high unemployment, high crime rates, and decaying buildings. Gary was founded in 1906 by the *United States Steel Cooperation*, which built a new steel mill here and named it after its chairman Gary. Gary is still an important steel town today, but rationalization in steel production has resulted in the layoff of many steelworkers. While the white middle class moved to the suburbs, unemployed black steelworkers remained in the city, where today, African-Americans make up over 80 percent of the population. As in Detroit, Gary, the city's former main train station, is not in good shape.

Shortly after the city was founded, the station was built by the architect M.A. Lang in the then modern neoclassical style inspired by the Chicago World Fair. There were already enough tracks here on the south shore of Lake Michigan not far from Chicago. Because the steel company wanted to sell steel to the construction industry, the station was built in the then-revolutionary technique of reinforced concrete construction, despite its conservative architectural style. This stable construction is probably also one reason why the station building - which was abandoned empty half a century ago, has since lost all its windows and doors due to vandalism, and has been devastated inside - is still standing.

In the US television documentary *Life After People*, the Union Station was shown as an example of how buildings that are left to decay develop within 30 years.

Gary Union Station (Photo: Wikipedia)

⊙ Redwood Falls and the department store founder

Redwood Falls is a small town in southern Minnesota, not far from the waterfalls of the Redwood River. In the 1880s, Richard W. Sears came to Redwood Falls as a station agent. Although still a teenager, Sears had to take a job as a telegrapher on the *Minnesota and St. Louis Railroad* to support his family after the death of his father. He improved his income as a stationmaster by trading coal and wood. In 1886, a load of pocket watches arrived at the station. At that time, it was common practice for companies to send goods to retailers without an order, and then to say that the return was unfortunately only possible under great circumstances. Yet, the Redwood Falls jeweler was fed up with such practices and refused to accept the watches. Sears saw an opportunity and asked the watch manufacturer if they could sell the watches themselves. Sears founded the *Richard W. Sears Watch Company*, advertised his watches to other railway employees - which could be ordered by letter - and surprisingly quickly sold all the watches. He ended up making a tidy profit. Finally, Sears hired watchmaker Alvah C. Roebuck to repair broken watches that were returned. In 1887, Sears published its first catalog. In it, watches and jewelry were offered. Later editions soon included bicycles, shoes, and saddles. And in 1894, the catalog - the company was now called *Sears, Roebuck and Co.* - was already 322 pages thick. The Sears & Roebuck catalog became a US consumer legend, and the company soon became the largest retailer in the US. Today, the company's headquarters are in Chicago, where the Sears Tower - at times the tallest building in the world - bore the name of the company, which started out of a train station. Since July 2009, the building has been re-named Willis Tower.

⊙ The Kipton railway accident

Kipton is a village not far from Lake Erie in the northern part of the state of Ohio, with about 270 inhabitants. A railway line, which once belonged to the *Lake-Shore Railway*, runs through the village. In April 1891, a fast mail train collided head-on with a passenger train at Kipton station, killing 6 postal workers and 2 engineers, and causing severe damage to the station. The cause of the accident was thought to be a clock that had stopped for 4 minutes and then continued running. Unaware of the wrong time, the driver of the passenger train arrived at the passing point too late. After the accident, the railway company hired the well-known Cleveland jeweler and watchmaker Webb C. Ball as a time inspector to establish standards of precision and a system for checking railway clocks.

He established strict guidelines for the manufacture of watches used by the railway. By the end of his career, Ball was responsible for the railway watch inspection system throughout North America. From his Cleveland jewelry business, the *Ball Watch Company* was born, which today has its headquarters in Switzerland. In the USA, people still say "on the Ball" when they mean an exact time.

The Midway Station

In St. Paul, Minnesota, there is the Amtrak Midway Station (117,000 passengers in 2013). This station is so named because it is located in the Midway district. Additionally, the district takes its name from its location in the middle between the two city centers of the dual city of Minneapolis-St. Paul. The name fits in yet another sense. The train station and the district are located at 45 degrees latitude, exactly in the middle between the equator and the North Pole.

☉ The restaurant in Topeka railway station

In 1876, railroad employee Fred Harvey set up a restaurant in the Topeka (Kansas) train station. A year earlier, he had opened two cafés on the *Kansas Pacific Railway* and realized the need for decent dining facilities in the railroad environment. At that time, these were anything but self-evident in the harsh West of the USA. The railroads hired Harvey to create more modern restaurants, creating the world's first restaurant chain 8 decades before McDonald's. Harvey further developed the systemized gastronomy with standardized uniforms for female waiters and waitresses, thus creating the "Harvey Girl." After some initial hesitation, he also managed railway dining cars and eventually set up hotels (many of which still exist today, albeit under a different name). Part of Harvey's secret of success was the richness of his food at reasonable prices. His last words on his deathbed are said to have been, "Boys, don't cut the ham too thin."

St. Louis Union Station

Several US railway stations built around the turn of the century adopted European architectural models. Yet, Union Station in St. Louis surpassed them all as its architecture was based on an entire city: the crenelated Carcassonne in southern France. The Union Station in St. Louis was opened in 1894. The architect was the German-born Theodore Link. It was once considered the busiest and largest railway station in the world (32 tracks). In the 1940s, the station still counted 100,000 passengers and visitors per day. In 1948, the American President Truman left for Washington from here. A famous photo shows him holding a newspaper in his hand, predicting his election defeat, but Truman won the election. In the 1950s, the railways in the USA finally went downhill rapidly, and in 1978, the last train left this station. After a $150 million renovation, a hotel was opened in the station in 1985, followed by a shopping center and entertainment facilities.

From Amshack to Gateway Station

The modest provisional Amtrak station of St. Louis, which served as a train stop after the closure of Union Station, was ridiculed by the population as *Amshack*. This makeshift station lasted for 26 years until Amtrak moved to another temporary location in 2004. Finally, in November 2008, a new intermodal station, the *St. Louis Gateway Transportation Center*, was opened, linking intercity rail, light rail, Greyhound buses, and transit buses.

Kansas City Union Station

The Kansas City Union Station, built in 1914, was closed in the 1980s for rail traffic - although passenger trains stop here again today - but was extensively renovated in 1996-1999. It now serves cultural purposes and as a railway museum. This was financed by a special tax, which the citizens of Kansas and Missouri (Kansas City is in the state of Missouri) approved in a vote. By the way, the huge clock in the train station hall is still a popular meeting place in the city today ("meet me under the clock").

However, during the renovation, the traces of a shooting were left intact, which brought the station dubious fame in 1933. When the police accompanied a criminal - who was arrested in another city and was to be transferred by train - from the station to the police car, his accomplice suddenly opened fire on the police. Four policemen and the criminal died in the hail of bullets. The public was so shocked that a relatively small police agency was expanded into the FBI as a result.

Kansas City Union Station (Bild: Wikipedia)

⊙ Calmar (Iowa) and Anton Dvorak

The Czech composer Anton Dvorak (1814-1874) was considered a railway fan. He often went to Prague Main Station to write down the vehicle numbers of passing locomotives. A job in the USA was made palatable to him by the fact that he was told that he could then observe the locomotives of the New York station. In 1892, he took up the post of director of the National Conservatory of Music in New York. Yet, New York disappointed him because, at that time, it was not possible to watch trains at all in the Grand Central Depot. At least during his three-year stay in the US, he had the opportunity to get to know the American railway system during his trips to the village of Spillville, Iowa, where he spent his summer holidays. However,

Spillville did not have a railway station, so Dvorak and his family had to change to the carriage at the Calmar station 6 kilometers away. In 1895, Dvorak returned to Prague. In early 1904, he went to the Prague railway station to watch trains. He returned to his apartment with a cold. A short time later, the composer and locomotive fan died.

Omaha - the city of beautiful train stations

The inconspicuous prairie city of Omaha has had several outstanding railway station buildings in the course of its history. When Burlington Station was opened in 1898 as part of a world exhibition in Omaha, its architecture attracted visitors from all over the world. A German commission even voted the station building, with its neoclassical column portico, the most beautiful train station in America. A renovation between 1929 and 1930 adapted the building to the changing tastes of the time in order to compete with the Art Deco style of the Union Station under construction. In 1985, when the four chandeliers in the counter hall were taken down, one broke and had to be sold in pieces. After 2005, the station building was finally converted into a luxury apartment building and marketed as *The Burlington*. There seems to be money for this in Omaha. The city is also home to billionaire Warren Buffet, also known as the "Oracle of Omaha."

Omaha - Union Station

The Union Station of Omaha, Nebraska, is considered one of the most beautiful buildings of the Art Deco style in the Midwest of the USA. The station building, completed in 1931, is clad in cream-colored terracotta bricks. The architect Gilbert Stanley Underwood intended the building to reflect the power and masculinity of the railway. However, in 1971, the train station was closed to passenger traffic, and today it houses a museum. Above an entrance portal is an engraved quotation from Abraham Lincoln from 1832, which reads, "No other improvement can equal in utility the railroad."

The architectural quality of Omaha's railway stations is also recognized in the neighboring state of Wyoming. After renovation and conversion of the Cheyenne station into a railway museum, it is called "The most beautiful railroad station between Omaha and Sacramento."

Omaha Union Station Bahnhofshalle im Art Deco Stil
(Bild: Wikipedia)

⊙ Walt Disney and Marceline

Walt Disney (1901-1966) was born in Chicago. At the age of four, his family moved to a farm in the small town of Marceline, Missouri. There, Disney developed his love for drawing. Additionally, his weakness for the railway originates from his time in Marceline. The town is located at the important railway line Kansas City-Chicago, and Disney also worked for the railway for a while.

Later Disney said, when talking about Marceline, "To tell the truth, more things of importance happened to me in Marceline than have happened since or are likely to happen in the future."

When Walt Disney became established in Hollywood with his drawing studio, he built a large garden railway on his estate. His fondness for the railway was later also evident in the design of Disneyland in California. In 1959, the ALWEG monorail system developed in Germany by Alf Wenner Gren was used there for the first time, heralding the age of modern suspended railways. The Disneylands/worlds in the US also have classic stations with steam trains that transport visitors. The 19th-century American town, which is being recreated in the parks, resembles in many elements the town of Marceline, where Disney spent his childhood.

Hanlontown and the sunbeams

Hanlontown is a very small town (only 229 inhabitants in 2000) in the north of the flat prairie state of Iowa. In such a place without much layering, architecture, or spectacular scenery, it is not easy to find something special, a unique selling point to attract attention, tourists, and visitors. At first, Hanlontown tried "pork days" because, after all, pigs are bred there. Yet, the success was limited because there are many "Pig Days" in the Midwest, and in Des Moines, the capital of Iowa, there is even a world pig show. Apart from a water tower and a few grain silos, there was nothing architecturally remarkable in this small town. Additionally, the train station was long ago closed down. However, the dead straight tracks connecting Iowa with Minneapolis continued to run through the town. Finally, they found something special, something that many inhabitants had observed for a long time without paying any further attention. At the solstice on June 21, the sun sets exactly between the rails (these are inclined like the earth's axis by 23 degrees from the north-south axis). Thus, the sunset festival was created in Hanlontown, and every year a large part of the population of the town plus a few visitors on folding chairs watch the sun go down exactly between the tracks and make them shine.

Britt and the Hobos

The small town of Britt (2000 inhabitants), also located in northern Iowa, owes its existence to the construction of a railway line, whose station was the lifeblood of the town for a long time. The town has also come up with something special. The local Chamber of Commerce organizes the *National Hobo Convention* every August. The National Hobo Convention is the largest gathering of tramps and hobos, people who ride illegally on rail freight trains. There's even a Hobo Museum in Britt. Whether the well-organized event reflects the outsider and freedom-loving attitudes of the early hobos is a matter of debate.

The North Platte Canteen

North Platte is a Nebraska railroad town on the North Platte River, served by the Union Pacific Railroad. An important east-west railway connection of the USA runs through the small town, which had a lot of passenger traffic during the Second World War. Between December 1941 and April 1946, more than six million US soldiers traveled through the town (from the east to the west coast and thus to the Pacific front and vice versa). At that time, trains were still pulled by steam locomotives, and in North Platte, they had to take a ten-minute break to pick up water and lubricate the wheels. This short stop at North Platte station was intended to give the Midwest an opportunity to show its hospitality. Rae Wilson, a young woman, wrote to the local newspaper suggesting that a kind of canteen be set up in the station for soldiers passing through. She contacted friends and businessmen, and on December 22nd, 1941, a canteen committee was set up. Already on December 25th, Christmas Day, the work could begin. Young women handed out snacks - prepared by volunteers from North Platte and the surrounding area - and small gifts to the 3000-5000 soldiers who traveled through North Platte daily.

Finally, they even got permission from the railway company to use the former dining hall of the station for the "canteen." In April 1946, the North Platte Canteen was closed, but many soldiers remembered this ray of hope for a long time. With the decline in rail passenger traffic, the Union Pacific station was demolished in 1973. However, a plaque on bricks of the demolished station building now commemorates the former North Platte Canteen on the site where the station building once stood.

America's economic barometer

North Platte has one more special feature in terms of railroading. Here is the Bailey Yard of the Union Pacific Railroad Company. It is considered the largest marshaling yard in the world. On an area of 11 km^2, the track length is more than 500 km. 2600 people are employed in the marshaling yard. 135 trains and more than 10,000 wagons are shunted here every day. Theses numbers reflect what America imports, exports, and consumes. No wonder that Bailey Yard is considered the *economic barometer of America.*

Newton and Shakespeare

In the city of Newton, Kansas (17,000 inhabitants), founded in the 1870s, two Englishmen are remembered. Firstly, the name of the city refers to the natural scientist Isaac Newton. On the other hand, the architecture of the city's three-gable railway station, built in 1930, was modeled on Shakespeare's house in Stratford-upon-Avon. This civilized relationship is in contrast to the city's former reputation. After 8 men were killed in a shoot-out in Newton in 1871, the city was considered bloody, lawless, and the most wicked in the West. However, when the Santa Fe Railway set up an operating base in this centrally located town, the city grew rapidly and consolidated, including in terms of security.

⊙ Hope and Bill Clinton

Actually, the small town of Hope in Arkansas is rather a place in the South. Bill Clinton, the US president from 1993-2001, was born here. In 1995, a visitor center was therefore set up in the town's railway station, which opened in 1917, and also includes a small Clinton museum.

2.9 The Southern States

⊙ Nashville Union Station and Al Capone

The neo-Romanesque-Gothic style Union Station of Nashville, Tennessee, opened in 1900, is one of the most striking US railway station buildings with its tall clock tower. Since 1986, the former station building has housed a hotel. In 1932, the station had a prominent passenger. The gangster Al Capone (1899-1947), who had become rich in Chicago with illegal alcohol trade (prohibition was in effect), was led through the station in handcuffs. He was on his way to Alcatraz, where he was imprisoned from 1932.

⊙ The station of Tutwiler and the Blues

The African-American W.C. (William Christoper) Handy (1873-1958) is also called the "Father of the Blues." Handy was the son of freed slaves. His faithful parents enrolled him for organ lessons, but Handy preferred to play the guitar. Starting in 1903, he fronted a band in Clarksdale, Mississippi. In 1903, Handy was waiting for a train in Tutwiler, not far from Clarksdale, which was several hours late. He was trying to sleep on a bench on the platform when he was awoken by an unknown black singer who repeated the line, "Going where the Southern cross the Dog" (Southern and Yazoo Delta Railroad, nicknamed "The Yellow Dog," are two railroad lines in the region). To do so, he elicited strange sounds from his guitar by pressing a knife on the strings. The train station of Tutweiler is thus considered the place where Handy heard the blues for the first time. In 1906, Handy moved to Memphis and developed the style further. The Tutwiler station building no longer exists today. However, there are freight sheds along the tracks, which are decorated with murals commemorating the memorable encounter in 1903 and the emergence of the blues in Tutwiler station.

☉ Muddy Waters and the Blues Station

Another important station for the history of the blues is Clarksdale, about 100 kilometers south of Memphis. Clarksdale markets itself as the birthplace and world capital of the blues. From the city and its surroundings came musicians like Muddy Waters, Sam Cooke, and John Lee Hooker. Clarksdale was also an important station on the Illinois Central Railway, which ran straight north to Chicago. When cotton-picking machines were introduced in 1946, many black cotton pickers became unemployed, and the railroad sucked rural African-Americans into Chicago like a vacuum cleaner. Additionally, blues musicians went this way. Some got off the train in Memphis, but blues musician Muddy Waters was heading from this station for Chicago in 1943.

Today, the former Clarksdale train station, which houses a bistro, is a warehouse converted into the Delta Blues Museum (the Clarksdale area is also called the Delta, although it is several hundred miles from the Mississippi Delta), and the Greyhound Bus Station form the Blues Alley in Clarkdale's historic blues district.

☉ Johnny Cash and the Amqui Station

The American country singer Johnny Cash (1932-2003) was considered a railway fan. In 1979, he purchased the disused train station in Amqui, a suburb of the community of Madison near Nashville. He had the lightweight station building transported on a flatbed truck to his estate in the Nashville suburb of Hendersonville, where he restored and exhibited it in his collection of railway memorabilia. The result was a mini-museum. After Cash's death in 2003, a foundation purchased the building and donated it to the Madison community. The community returned it to its original location in 2006, and restoration work began in 2008. The station, which is no longer used by passenger trains, is to be converted into a visitor center that will provide information about the history of the Madison railroad.

Chattanooga Choo Choo

In 1941, the big band swing song "Chattanooga Choo Choo" from the movie *Sun Valley Serenade*, in which Glen Miller and his orchestra played, reached number 1 in US sales. The commercial version of the song was the first in the USA to be awarded a gold record (over 1 million copies sold). The melody of the song was also used several times for German songs, for example, in 1983 for Udo Lindenberg's "Special Train to Pankow."

The term Chattanooga Choo Choo is slang for a steam train that travels towards the southern states. The town of Chattanooga, located in Tennessee, was an important railway junction at that time. Many trains heading south passed through the town. However, the last passenger train stopped in Chattanooga in the early 1970s, and there were plans to demolish the town's train station. However, it was eventually decided to use the fame that song brought to Chattanooga and turn the railway facilities into a tourist attraction. This is one of the most popular attractions in Tennessee today. The station building has been converted into a Holiday Inn Hotel, and it is even possible to stay overnight in railroad cars converted into hotel rooms. The American Model Railroad Association also has its headquarters on the railroad grounds, where it has the largest model railroad layout in the USA.

Richmond Broad Street Station

The architecture of Broad Street Station in Richmond, Virginia, is reminiscent of the Pantheon in Rome and also of the Jefferson Memorial in Washington. The resemblance between the buildings is no surprise considering that the

Pantheon was the model (also for Washington Union Station), and the architect Pope also designed the Jefferson Memorial in Washington, inaugurated in 1943. In Richmond, there is another architecturally interesting station, Main Street Station.

⊙ Biltmore Station and the billionaire

In the 19th century, the American Cornelius Vanderbilt laid the foundation stone for the fortune of the billionaire family Vanderbilt with steamships and railways. His grandson, George W. Vanderbilt II (1862-1914), was more of a connoisseur of the arts than an entrepreneur, leaving the management of the Vanderbilt companies to his brothers. In 1888, he and his mother visited an area in western North Carolina. He liked it so much that he decided to build an estate near the town of Asheville.

The Biltmore House, which was built there between 1888 and 1895, following the model of a Loire castle, is still the largest private house in the US. It has 250 rooms with a total living space of 16,300 m^2 and is today a tourist attraction with more than one million visitors per year. For the many servants, Vanderbilt had his own small town built opposite of the estate, for which he bought up the small village of Best (today the town is called Biltmore Village and belongs to the city of Asheville). Since 1880, Best already had its own railway station, but when Vanderbilt took over the village, he had the station demolished. The architect Richard Morris Hunt built a new, more representative station, although it still looks modest compared to Biltmore Estate.

It was here that important visitors arrived, including US presidents, who Vanderbilt invited to his estate.

Until 1975, the Biltmore station was in operation as Southern Railway Passenger Depot. Today the station building houses a restaurant.

69

New Orleans and the separate rooms

Built in 1954, the New Orleans Passenger Terminal was considered ultramodern when it opened. Nevertheless, the station had one retrograde element: separate waiting areas for white and "colored" passengers. This separation was still widespread in the Southern states in the 1950s, under so-called Jim Crow laws, which prescribed racial segregation. In 2005, Hurricane Katrina spared the station for the most part, and it was used as a temporary substitute prison.

☞ A special feature of this station: the track ballast consists of shells from seashells.

The station of Texarkana

Texarkana is a city that lies exactly on the border of the states of Texas and Arkansas. Thus there is a Texarkana, Arkansas, and a Texarkana, Texas. The station is located on the territory of the state of Arkansas. When a *Texas Eagle* train southbound stops at the station, the front cars are in Texas, and the rear cars are in Arkansas.

The beautiful station of Greensboro

The Greensboro station in North Carolina, built in 1927, is one of the most beautiful in the southern US with its neoclassical portico. It is also an example of how to bring the train back to the city center. In 1979, the Southern Railway, which had no interest in passenger transport, donated the building to the city. From then on, passengers had to wait for trains in a freight station on the outskirts of the city. However, the city and state later renovated the station, and in 2005, the station became a regular Amtrak stop again.

⊙ Key Wests Rail across the water

At the beginning of the 20th century, there were plans in the United States for a fast, direct connection to the Panama Canal via Mexico. This was to be achieved using railway lines through Central America, Cuba, and Florida, with the shortest possible sea connections. In the US, the aim was to build a railway line to the southernmost point, the Key West Islands in Florida, from where it was not far to Cuba. Financed by the industrialist H.M. Flagler, the construction of the Miami (Homestead)-Key West line started in 1905. In 1912, the line was completed, connecting and crossing the Key West chain of islands with numerous bridges. Key West thus had a terminal, and became the most important transshipment port south of Richmond, Virginia, and was nicknamed "Gibraltar of America."

Flagler died a year later and did not have to experience what would happen to his railroad two decades later. On September 2, 1935, a hurricane occurred, with wind speeds reaching 200 km/h. 60 km of the track was destroyed, and over a section of 10 km, all traces of the railway line were wiped out by the storm. A 3 km long section of the track was even carried 30 km away by the wind to another beach. The railway line was never rebuilt, and a highway was built over what remained. However, part of the destroyed wooden railway station Key West Terminus was later rebuilt and now serves as the *Flagler Station Oversea Railway Historeum* museum.

⊙ Warm Springs and Franklin D. Roosevelt

Franklin Delano Roosevelt, US President from 1933-1945, fell ill with polio in 1921. He sought relief from his suffering in the warm mineral springs of Warm Springs, Georgia, among other places, to which he traveled by train from Washington. He was there so often that he had a white wooden house built for himself in Warm Springs, which was soon named the *Little White House* in allusion to Washington. Roosevelt died here in April 1945, shortly before the end of the war, and the black-decorated funeral procession to Washington started its journey in the small train station of Warm Springs, which was overflowing with mourners and onlookers that day.

Louisville Union Station

A list of station buildings worth seeing in the Southern States would not be complete without the Louisville Union Station with its glass mosaic windows, opened in 1891. It was once considered the largest station in the southern US.

Birmingham's exotic railway station

The demolition of the old station of Birmingham, the steel city of Alabama, is regarded by some as a bitter loss of valuable station architecture. The station was built in 1909, in a strange Byzantine-Turkish style, and with its round dome and 40 m high towers on each side, it resembled a cross between a basilica and a mosque. As was customary in the "deep south," it had separate waiting areas for "whites" and for "coloreds." In 1969, the station was demolished to make way for a smaller but more modern complex with offices and a hotel. However, the new building was never realized, and the vacated area was used to build a highway. The original railway station, which did not necessarily fit in with the architecture of the southern states, was thus replaced by an urban nothing.

Last train to Clarksville

The Monkees were an American pop quartet that was put together for the television series "The Monkees" in 1966. The Monkees' debut single in 1966 was "Last Train to Clarksville." The first verse went like this:

> *Take the last train to Clarksville,*
> *And I'll meet you at the station.*
> *You can be there by four-thirty,*
> *cause I made your reservation.*

The last verse was:

> *Take the last train to Clarksville,*
> *Now I must hang up the phone.*
> *I can't hear you in this noisy*
> *Railroad station all alone.*
> *And I don't know if I'm ever coming home.*

Since then, music fans wonder which Clarksville was meant since there are several cities with this name in the US. It is speculated that the station of Clarksville, Tennessee, inspired the song. However, the lyricist Bobby Hart said that he first thought of Clarksdale, Arizona, where he often spent his summer holidays, but then found that Clarksville sounded better in the song. Later, they would have found out that there was an airbase near Clarksville, Tennessee, which could have fit the story of the lyrics, yet, an anti-war song (it was released during the Vietnam War) would not have been intended.

Matewan and the miners

Matewan is a small mining town (500 inhabitants) in West Virginia, which was the scene of a bloody feud between the Hatfield family and the McCoy clan between 1878 and 1891, which made national headlines and killed over a dozen people.

In 1920 there was another bloody argument, the Battle of Matewan. This shootout was preceded by efforts by local miners to form a union. This did not please the local mine company and so they hired the Baldwin Felts detective agency to kick the miners out of their factory apartments. The local police chief did not like this procedure and issued an arrest warrant for the detectives arriving by train. On May 19, 1920, the chief of police Sid Hatfield, accompanied by miners, and the detectives, who in turn issued an order to arrest the chief of police, met at Matewan station. Eventually the mayor was called in, who found, however, that the detective's arrest warrant was a fake. Suddenly there was a shot, and it was never clarified who released it. In the shootout that followed, 7 detectives, 2 miners and the mayor Testerman were killed. A year later, the surviving detectives took revenge by shooting police chief Sid Hatfield. A museum is housed in the train station in Matewan, which provides information about the feud, the Matewan shootout and the great flood that led to the construction of a flood protection wall around the city, which is decorated with motifs from the eventful city history.

☞In 1987 the shootout was filmed. However, the film, titled Matewan, was shot in Thurmond, a small town in West Virginia that has maintained a 1920s atmosphere even better than Matewan.

Texas Crush Station

In the 1890s, the *Missouri, Kansas & Texas Railroad* was in the process of replacing older locomotives with newer, more powerful models. More than 50 old locomotives were no longer in use. This gave railway employee William G. Crush the idea of putting two of the obsolete locomotives on the tracks and racing them towards each other until they crashed, as a means to get rid of them. Something similar had been done months earlier near Cleveland.

Near Waco, Texas, four miles of tracks were laid, and the locomotives were prepared for the crash. The publicity drum started to do its job as more than 20,000 spectators were expected. Due to the event, a special station was built, called Crush, Texas. The event was scheduled for September 15th, 1896. 40,000 spectators arrived, and Crush became the second largest town in Texas for a short while. At five o'clock in the afternoon, the locomotives were lined up for a photoshoot at the point of collision and then slowly pulled in two different directions. Finally, the locomotives were put into operation, the drivers jumped off, and the locomotives raced towards each other at 70 km/h with five wagons in tow. Although safety had been tested beforehand, an unexpected event occurred: the steam boilers of both locomotives exploded, and metal parts flew through the air. Three spectators were killed, six were seriously injured, the official photographer lost an eye, and Crush lost his job. However, he was rehired the very next day. Today, a memorial plaque commemorates the event, but there are no traces of the Crush station anymore.

⊙Dallas Union Station and the assassination of Kennedy

The elegant Union Station in Dallas, with its neoclassical architecture, is one of the most beautiful railway station buildings in North America (in contrast to the station building in Houston, which was ridiculed as "Amshack"). It was built in 1916 and replaced five stations in the greater Dallas area. The station has nine platforms, and before World War II, it saw about 100 passenger trains per day, a number that declined rapidly in the 1950s. There were two signal towers north and south of the reception building, where traffic was controlled. On November 22, 1963, John F. Kennedy's motorcade reached Dealey Plaza (named after the editor of the *Dallas Morning News*, who had advocated for the construction of the station), not far from one of the signal towers. After the assassination of Kennedy, the police also interrogated the railway employees in the signal tower near the Plaza.

Galveston and the flood

In 1900, the Texan coastal town of Galveston, located on an island, was completely flooded by a hurricane. 8,000 people died, which is the biggest natural disaster in the history of the USA. At that time, 85 passengers, whose train was on a ferry from Houston to Galveston, also died.

The station opened in 1887, and its red brick building, which was considered the pride of Galveston, was also flooded.

As a result of the catastrophe, the ground level of the city, which was only 2.7 m above sea level, was raised by over 5 m, and a protective wall was built. In 1932, a new Art Deco station was opened. However, already in 1967, the last passenger trains left here. Today, ghostly plaster figures in the former waiting area recall the days of passenger railroading in Galveston.

⊙ Lubbock and Buddy Holly

Lubbock is an isolated city in the west of Texas. It is a long way from the other metropolitan areas of the USA.

It is, therefore, no surprise that the city's most famous son, the rock 'n' roll musician Buddy Holly (1936-1959), was more likely to travel by plane, which is why there is no real station anecdote about Buddy Holly. Yet, flying was not very safe in the fifties. On February 3, 1959, the small plane in which Buddy Holly and two other musicians were on, as they headed to a gig, crashed near Mason City, Iowa. This accident, in which all passengers died, went down in music history as "The Day the Music Died."

In Lubbock, the train station - which was built in the 1930s, closed in the early 1950s, and had served as a warehouse and restaurant - was bought by the city a few years ago and turned into the Buddy Holly Center. A connection between Buddy Holly and the local train station was thus finally established.

⊙ El Paso and Pancho Villa

The El Paso Union Depot was built in 1905-1906 by Daniel Burnham, the architect of Washington's Union Station, in the Classical Revival style. The building includes a tower with a pointed roof, reminiscent of a church steeple. When the Mexican folk hero Pancho Villa (1877-1923) escaped from a prison in Mexico City in 1913 (he had sawed through the iron bars of the window while a folk song was being sung loudly in the street), and fled from the Mexican government troops to Texas, he found accommodation in a cheap hotel in El Paso. During his time in Texas, Villa is said to have used the station tower as a lookout to prepare an attack on the neighboring Mexican town of Juarez.

Today the station is scarcely used. Two trains stop here per day, and on average of only 26 passengers on board.

⊙ Newman and the revolutionaries

Not far from El Paso lies Newman. Here, in 1915, the Mexican revolutionaries Victoriano Huerta and Pascual Orozco were arrested. Huerta had boarded a train in New York and claimed to be going to San Francisco. In reality, he planned to get off the train in Newman (the town is in Texas, and the station is in New Mexico), not far from the Mexican border, and meet Orozco, who had weapons with him. Both planned to travel on to Mexico and overthrow the president. However, the Americans had got wind of the operation, and the plans were thwarted.

Kirby and the Hobos

The small town of Kirby is also called the *hobo capital of Texas.* The marshaling yard of the Southern Pacific Railroad, located in the city, has contributed to this. There is also a railway bridge which offers protection from the rain.

San Antonio's old train station

The architect Harvey L. Page called the *International and Great Northern Depot of San Antonio*, which he designed and built in 1908, "my Tadj Mahal." The architecture of the station was strongly influenced by examples of the Spanish missionary style present in San Antonio. Yet, one stylistic element did not fit in. Instead of a cross or an angel as on a church building, the top of the dome is crowned by anNative-American who shoots an arrow towards the northeast. Today, there is a bank in the former station building, and the ticket offices have become bank counters. The bank that renovated the station had the right to place its logo in the large rose window in the front but then decided to restore the old *International and Great Northern* logo.

Fort Worth TP Station

The *Texas and Pacific Railroad Passenger Station of Fort Worth* is an impressive eleven-story Art Deco building that opened in 1931. The luxurious entrance hall is covered with marble floors, and the ceiling is decorated with filigree Art Deco patterns. Since 1958, an elevated road cut off the railway station from the city center, but the station went downhill and was closed in 1967. Yet, this was not its last word, as the station was renovated in 1999, and in 2001, it was connected to the *Trinity Rail Express*, the local rail service to the nearby city of Dallas. The ugly elevated street in front of the station was demolished in 2002, and the upper floors of the station were converted into luxury apartments.

⊙ **Austin and the poet**

The American writer André G. Dubus III (best known for his work *House of Sand and Fog*) began his studies at Bradford College in Massachusetts, where his father, also a writer, taught. At the age of 19, Dubus developed a difficult love affair with an Iranian student. To get over the relationship, he decided to move his place of study as far west as possible. He hence enrolled at various colleges west of the Mississippi. He bought a train ticket to visit each of these universities. When he got off at the Austin station, he saw a poster with delicious Mexican food, Texas beer, a cactus, and a beautiful senorita. Thus he got hooked again, and he decided to stay in Austin.

2.11 The Rocky Mountains States

Ogden and Promontory Point

Ogden, in the state of Utah, is an important railway junction in the western US. Not far from Ogden is the Promontory Summit. Here, on May 10, 1869, a golden spike was ceremonially hammered in to close the gap between the Union Pacific and Central Pacific networks, thus creating the first transcontinental connection in the USA.

Ogden, the nearest town, also benefited from the closure of this gap. Yet, in the decades that followed, Ogden was to become a dangerous place. Given the city's reputation, gangster Al Capone said in the 1920s that Ogden was far too rough for him. However, Ogden's Union Station, opened in 1924, provides a peaceful entrance to the city; in its missionary style, it looks like a neo-Romanesque basilica. Today, the station houses a railway museum.

The Lamar railway station

In 1866, prospective town planners asked the wealthy livestock owner A.R. Black if he would be willing to give up a portion of his pasture located at Blackwell Station to build a town. Although he was offered compensation and was to continue to own the land, Black refused. Even when they threatened to close the station, he refused. In response, the prospectors simply tore down the station and moved it 5 kilometers to the west. The demolition squad threw the Blackwell station sign into the dust and placed a sign in the new station with the inscription "Lamar." The station became the foundation of the new city. Lamar was named after the then Secretary of the Interior of the USA.

Cheyenne Depot

The railway station of Cheyenne, Wyoming, built in 1887 in a Richardsonian Romanesque style by Henry van Brunt, was once considered "the most beautiful railroad station between Omaha and Sacramento." Its dominating clock tower is strongly reminiscent of a church tower but also of a campanile. Today, the spacious station complex houses a railway museum.

⊙ Hilton and the train station of San Antonio (N.M.)

The hotel founder Conrad N. Hilton, son of a Norwegian immigrant, was born in San Antonio, New Mexico, in 1887. The Hiltons lived in a house near the train station, which also housed a shop. In 1906, when business was not going so well, they converted six rooms into guest rooms. Hilton worked all day in the shop, and at 1:00 a.m., he would go to the train station, where long-distance trains stopped, and ask passengers getting off if they needed accommodation. A room with breakfast cost $2.50. Through this experience, Hilton gained useful insights into the hotel business. In 1919, Hilton tried to buy shares at a bank in Cisco, Texas, after an interplay as a New Mexico State Representative and a soldier in World War I. As the negotiations dragged on, Hilton had to stay overnight, but unfortunately found that all hotels were fully booked. This led him to buy a hotel instead of a bank. Hilton was lucky with this investment, and soon he started to expand. In 1954, Hilton bought the Statler hotel group for over 100 million dollars and became one of the leading hoteliers in the world. In 1966, Conrad Hilton handed over the business to his son Barron Hilton. He is the grandfather of the starlet Paris Hilton and reportedly is unhappy with her excessive media presence (her presence though declined in the last decade).

⊙ Myrna Loy and the small station

The US actress Myrna Loy (1905-1993) was born in Radersburg, Montana as the daughter of an American politician. Her father is said to have come up with her first name when he was traveling through the USA by train, and the train stopped at a station called Myrna. This seems to be a legend because Myrna is a very common Irish-Gaelic girl's name, which means "the popular," while a station called Myrna cannot be found in the US.

☞By the way, Loy's birthplace Radersburg is located near Montana's capital Helena and thus not far from the town of Butte, whose train station houses a TV station today. This has been commented with "from train station to TV station, once station, always station."

The fountain at Reno station

Reno, Nevada, was once considered the gambling capital of the world but lost that title to Las Vegas in the 1960s. Unlike Las Vegas, however, Reno still has a train station. In 2006, Amtrak was even able to reopen the downtown train station, built in the 1920s and recently renovated, after a $280 million investment to lower the tracks in the city area, thus eliminating eleven intersections conflicting with road traffic. A large fountain was also installed in the entrance hall of the station. In October 1908, a Christian women's association, which wanted to combat alcohol consumption, had this 5-meter-high fountain erected in the center of Reno so that the men did not have to go into the saloons to drink. Similar fountains were also built in other cities in the country at that time.

2.12 The West Coast

Seattle King Street Station

Many American stations built around the turn of the century were based on European models in their eclectic historic architecture. The clock tower of King Street Station, opened in 1906 (which still has rail service today, unlike Union Station in Seattle, which is now an event center), is a copy of the bell tower in St. Mark's Square in Venice. This achievement is rather remarkable given that the Venetian Campanile no longer existed in 1906, as it collapsed in 1902 during an attempt to try to install an elevator. But in the year 1912, 1000 years after the building of the first tower started, the Campanile was rebuilt, and the station tower in Seattle had its model again.

Portland (Oregon) - Go by train

The Union Station building in Portland, Oregon, is characterized by a very high clock tower, on which the motto "GO BY TRAIN" can be read. Perhaps this slogan has had an unconscious effect on the attitudes of the population because Portland is considered an un-American compact, traffic-avoiding city. That is why it is nicknamed "Mecca of Antisprawl." In 1986, a modern light rail system was opened in Portland. In 2001, a tram was also introduced, and since 2005, the slogan "Go by streetcar" has been displayed on a building in downtown Portland, alluding to the slogan on the train station tower.

☞ Because of its breweries, Portland is, by the way, now also known as "Munich on the Willamette."

⊙ Palo Alto and Stanford's dream

Leland Stanford (1824-1893) was an American politician and railway magnate. He was a co-founder of the *Central Pacific Railroad*. His only son, Leland Stanford Junior, died at the age of 16 of a typhoid infection during a journey through Europe. In memory of his beloved and only son, Stanford founded the *Leland Stanford Junior University* in Palo Alto, a suburb of San Francisco (now part of Silicon Valley), connected to this city by a railway line. The university opened in 1891 and is now one of the world's leading higher education institutions. A mural in the Palo Alto train station building, which opened in 1940, spans the arc from Stanford's railroad activities to his dream of a university.

Today, the flat Palo Alto is also a city for cyclists. There are now bicycle parking garages at stations in California that are marketed under the name Bikestation. The largest, with 150 spaces, is located at the Caltrain Station in Palo Alto.

Davis and the cyclists

Another cycling city, at times considered the leader in North America in this respect, is the ecologically oriented university city of Davis. At the train station, the large number of bicycle racks is quite striking by American standards. The station was built in 1913 as a representative entrance to the university town in the then-modern Spanish missionary style.

Los Angeles Union Station

Built in 1939 in a mixture of Spanish colonial style and Art Deco, Los Angeles Union Station (acronym LAUS) is also nicknamed "*The last of America's great railway stations*."

And since Hollywood is not far away, Union Station later appeared in several movies, such as *Speed, Blade Runner*, and *Star Trek*. In the movie *Bladerunner*, the waiting area functioned as a police station.

With the decline of rail passenger transport after the Second World War, however, almost all long-distance traffic was lost. Today, however, because of the city's congested roads, the importance of the railway station is growing again - as a local traffic hub. With over 25,000 passengers a day, it now sees even more passengers than before the war, when there were only 7,000 a day.

⊙ Pasadena Union Station

While the Los Angeles Union Station provided a large stage for emerging stars and starlets through press photographers and interested audiences, the established stars usually got off the train one stop earlier to travel to Hollywood more discreetly. They did so at the Pasadena train station located on the eastern edge of the metropolitan area. Bette Davis once arrived here and was annoyed that no film studio employee was at the station to pick her up. However, a staff member had been at the station. She explained that she just did not see anyone who looked like a movie star getting off the train.

The Pasadena Union Station, which had been demolished to make way for a construction project, is now rebuilt in its original form.

☞At this station, Harpo Marx of the Marx Brothers, as a joke, got into the dining car of a waiting train, stole the menu from two ladies sitting at the table, tore it up, and put the pieces into his mouth. Then, one of the two ladies said to the waitress "please bring me a new menu, somebody has eaten mine."

San Diego Union Station

Because of strong immigration from Mexico and the rest of Latin America, a high birth rate of immigrants, and the fact that every other child born in California already has parents of Latin American origin (Hispanics/Latinos), there is sometimes speculation about a *Mexicanization* of California ("Mexifornia").

A hundred years ago, this perspective did not exist in the state. Yet, when the Victorian-style Union Station in San Diego was demolished in 1915 for the *Panama-California Exhibition* - which was to underpin the city's position as a port and transportation hub - it was replaced by a Spanish colonial-style building designed by two Anglo-American architects.

However, the honor of buying the first ticket was left to the last veteran of the US-Mexican War of 1846-1848, which was triggered by the US annexation of Texas. After the war, Mexico also lost territory, which became portions of the states of California, Nevada, New Mexico, and Arizona.

San Ysidro Transit Center

From San Diego´s Union Station, you can take the Blue Line of the light rail transit system to the San Ysidro Transit Center. The San Ysidro Transit Center is located at the border crossing with Mexico, which results in high passenger numbers, as the border crossing between San Diego and Tijuana is the busiest in the world with 30 million people per year. But you can cross the border by rail. Those who do not want to be stuck in traffic jams can cross the border on foot and board the light rail on the US side. By the way, San Diego was the first US city to introduce a new light rail system after the oil crisis (the first city in North America was Edmonton in 1978). In 1981, the first line opened (from the station to the border crossing at San Ysidro).

⊙ Michael Jackson´s residence as railway station

Michael Jackson was considered a train fan. In Linz, he wanted to buy the Grottenbahn, and he went to the castle Neuschwanstein by special train with himself as the only passenger. The main building of his Neverland Ranch, part of a former amusement park, was designed as a railway station, complete with railway tracks.

San Bernardino

The massive Spanish Mission Revival Style station building of San Bernardino in Southern California was the largest station building west of the Mississippi when it opened in 1918. The local newspaper wrote at the time that San Bernardino station would be "the best station in the entire West." At first, it was also very busy, but after the Second World War, passenger numbers declined rapidly. Today, the station has only 11,000 train passengers per year, but local rail traffic has been increasing in recent years.

Stuck in Lodi

In 1969, the US rock group Creedence Clearwater Revival released the album *Green River*, which contained the song "Lodi." It ended with the lines:

If I only had a dollar for every song I sung

You know I'd catch the train back to where I live

Oh! Lord, I am stuck in Lodi again.

It's not easy to get stuck in Lodi because the city has a train station from which trains still leave until this day.

3. Central America and the Caribbean

In Central America long-distance rail passenger transport does not really exist anymore. Buses dominate long-distance transport, and in Mexico, passenger transport by air has a certain importance. In contrast, modest long-distance rail traffic still exists in Cuba.

Mexico once had a relatively large rail network of over 30,000 km. Under Porfirio Díaz, President of the country from 1877-1880 and 1884-1911, Mexico was opened to foreign investment, and railway construction was even supported by government subsidies. In Mexico, therefore, there was a lively railway construction by American, British, and French companies around the turn of the century. There were also hundreds of trams and several plantation railways. But since Díaz invested little in education, the majority of the population remained poor and had little to do with rail transport. After the Second World War, road transport became more important than rail. At the end of the 1990s, the remaining railway companies were sold to North American freight railways, and the passenger traffic was closed.

However, freight transport is profitable due to the increasing economic integration between the United States and Mexico under the NAFTA agreement and the fact that both countries have the same railroad gauge (1435 mm, normal gauge).

In Central America, however, rail freight transport is less successful because the transport distances are shorter and the rail infrastructure is repeatedly damaged by natural disasters. This also hinders passenger traffic. Nevertheless, there are efforts to expand the latter in the capital regions of Costa Rica and El Salvador and to set up tourist trains.

Veracruz- the first railway station in Mexico

As early as 1837, a concession was awarded for the construction of the first Mexican railway line from the seaport of Veracruz to the capital Mexico City. In 1842, construction work began in Veracruz, and in 1850, the first steam train went to the Mexico City suburb of El Molino. However, the connection to the capital could not be opened until 1873. Thus, Veracruz was the first Mexican city to have a railway station. However, no passenger trains have departed from the station for a long time.

⊙ **Porfirio Diaz and the narrow-gauge railway**

The fact that many railway lines were built under the rule of dictator Porfirio Díaz was of particular benefit to him at the end of his reign. In 1911, after the beginning of the Mexican Revolution, President Díaz fled by rail from the capital to Veracruz, where he embarked for Europe. He began his journey at the San Lazaro train station in Mexico City.

At that time, two lines led from this station to the Caribbean coast: a standard gauge railway, the *Mexican Railway*, and a narrow-gauge railway, the *Interoceania*. Díaz deliberately chose the slower *Interoceania*, as he thought that any henchmen would suspect that he would take the faster standard gauge line. The presidential train was preceded by an empty train, and behind the train, a third train with security forces loyal to him followed. The San Lazaro station is no longer in operation. However, the symbol of the Mexico City subway station of the same name shows a steam locomotive, and thus reminds of the former station of the capital.

⊙ El Camaron and the treasury

In the revolutionary upheavals of the early 20th century, presidents in Mexico came and went quickly. According to an anecdote, a president secretly filled a railway carriage with the nation's wealth in order to take it abroad via Veracruz. The stations along the line were instructed by telegraph to set the railway points accordingly. However, the station manager of El Camaron was drinking tequila when the news arrived. He sent his assistant to fetch another bottle and set the points on the way back. But the train had already derailed. After all, it was a way to secure the national treasure.

Aguascalientes and the world heritage

The railway station of Aguascalientes (located in the state of the same name) was built in 1884. In 2001, Mexico proposed that the station and its extensive facilities, which are completely preserved in their 1890s' state, should be added as an industrial monument to the World Heritage List (however, to this day, they have not been included).

⊙ Nuevo Laredo and Garcia Marquez

The Colombian writer Gabriel Garcia Marquez (1927-2014) was forced out of the United States in 1961, as his work for the Cuban press office *Prensa Latina* in New York was no longer welcomed due to the Cuban revolutionaries' increasing shift to the left. He decided to settle in Mexico. He set foot on Mexican soil for the first time at the Nuevo Laredo station. From here, he took the train to Mexico City. The train station of Nuevo Laredo, long since closed for passenger traffic, is now called *Estacion Palabra Gabriel García Márquez* (Palabra = word) and houses a cultural center.

Mexico City - Buenavista and the good view

In 1873, a railway link from Buenavista Station in Mexico City to the seaport of Veracruz heralded the era of long-distance rail transport in Mexico. In 1892, a statue of Columbus was erected in the square in front of the station to mark the 400th anniversary of the discovery of America. The old station was demolished in 1958 to make room for office buildings. Not far from there, the Mexican president opened the architecturally rather unspectacular new Buena-vista station in 1961, which was probably inspired by Roma Termini.

The fact that the front of the station building was very wide was a coincidence because it had to bear the letters ESTACIÓN DE FERROCARRILES NACIONALES DE MEXICO.

Today, there is no longer a national railway company, and the station only bears the letters MEXICO BUENAVISTA. Buenavista means "good view," and in the beginning, this also meant seeing the spectacular, pointed skyscraper that rises not far from the station, as the 1971 film *Estación de Buenavista* shows on youtube). However, with increasing road traffic, the air in the Mexico City basin became worse and worse, and the view disappeared. In the last decade, however, an improvement was achieved by using lower-emission vehicles.

Buenavista and the suburban railway

Mexico's railways were privatized at the end of the 1990s. A short time later, the railroad passenger traffic was completely shut down. The new private companies, often US-owned, focused on profitable freight transport. Even the Buenavista Station, the largest station in the capital, did not see any passenger trains after January 2000.

However, since the city is choking from road traffic, the city's already large underground network is now being supplemented by suburban trains. In March 2008, the Mexican president personally opened the section to Buenavista-Lechria of the 27 km long railway line to Cuautitlán. The construction of the railway line was necessary because the existing tracks belong to a private railway company. 100 million passengers per year or almost 300,000 passengers per day were expected, which should have breathed new life into the Buenavista station. In June 2008, however, the number of passengers was only 30,000 per day, but by 2010, the number reached 200,000 per day.

⊙ Trotsky and the Lecheria Station

The painter Diego Rivera, who was married to the equally famous painter Frida Kahlo, was considered a communist.
Once, he was commissioned by Rockefeller to paint a wall at the Rockefeller Center in New York. Yet, when Rivera integrated a Lenin into the painting, Rockefeller was so annoyed that he had the painting completely destroyed.
After the revolutionary Trotsky fell out of favor in Russia, Rivera invited him to join him in Mexico in 1936. Trotsky arrived in Veracruz by ship and traveled by train to Mexico City. From there, he had to take a train to the suburb of Lecheria, where Rivera picked him up by car and took him to the house of his wife, Frida Kahlo.

⊙ Guanajuato and Diego Rivera

The Mexican painter Diego Rivera (1886-1957), who became famous for his wall paintings, was born in Guanajuato, where his family owned a silver mine. The following anecdote is about the birth of his sister. When the birth in the family home was imminent, they did not want to confront Rivera, who was a young boy at the time, directly with the birth process, and told him that he had to go to the train station, where his little sister would arrive in a box. He waited at the station hour after hour, but a box did not arrive. When he finally asked around, he was told that the baby had already arrived home. Back at his parents' house, he asked where the box was in which the baby had been delivered. Embarrassed, the relatives could only show him a shoe box. He ran out of the room and said they were all liars.

Guanajuato and the strange market hall

The silver city of Guanajuato has a strange market hall with a clock tower in the city center, which resembles a train station hall. There are two possible explanations for this resemblance. The first explanation states that only after building an elaborate railway station in the rich silver city, did the city administration realize that a railway connection could not be built due to the difficult topography of the city's landscape. A second explanation is that the hall was a railway station originally intended for use in a European city - but was eventually not used - and whose iron construction (or at least its design) was then installed in Guanajuato. The train station's original destination is said to have been either in Belgium or in Paris.

Guadalajara and the Tequila Express

Guadalajara, the second-largest city in Mexico, has neither long-distance nor suburban rail transport. Projects to connect Guadalajara with Mexico City (600 km away) by a high-speed rail line were also abandoned in 2006. The investment requirement for the project was calculated to be over five billion dollars, and it was concluded that cost-covering passenger figures could not be achieved. In 2014, a Mexico City-Queretaro high-speed rail project was commissioned (with later extension to Guadalajara), but the project, won by a Chinese consortium, was later canceled. However, since 1989, there has been an underground light rail system (length 24 km) in the city.

☞In 2006, when UNESCO declared the tequila production area near the city a World Heritage Site, a tourist train was set up, the *Tequila Express*, which offers an excursion to the tequila production area every weekend.

⊙ San Luis Potosi

San Luis Potosi is the capital of the Mexican state of the same name. The city has two train stations: *Central* and *Nacional*. The Central station was built in the 1920s, and its cubature even slightly resembles the Stuttgart main railway station built at the same time. The walls of the entrance hall are decorated with murals, which were painted in 1943 by the famous Mexican muralist Fernando Leal (1896-1964). One of the murals shows a map of the state of San Luis Potosi (whose inhabitants, by the way, think the state has the outline of a dog). Another picture shows a port scene with a ship unloading its cargo, yet San Luis Potosi is deep in the interior and, therefore, far away from any port. Today, the pictures are again admired by many visitors because a railway museum was opened in the railway station.

⊙ Julian Carrillo

The Mexican composer Julian Carrillo (1875-1965) was born in the village of Ahualulco and studied in San Luis Potosi. Carrillo was known and controversial for his theory of the "13th musical tone." However, San Luis Potosi was so proud of Carillo that his birthplace was temporarily renamed Ahualulco del Sonido 13 from 1932 to 1944. A railway station near San Luis Potosi, which has been closed for many years, was also named after him.

Cuautla and the old station building

The city of Cuautla, not far from Mexico City, used to be called the "city with the oldest station building in the world." The first station, located near the city center and opened in 1881, was built into the walls of a Dominican convent. The convent was constructed in 1657 but no longer in use. However, this old station has long since been replaced by a faceless station on the outskirts of the city. Yet, even there, no passenger trains stop anymore, and the "new" station is now closed.

Chapala and the lake

Not far from Guadalajara is Lake Chapala, the largest lake in Mexico. In the year 1926, the water of the lake rose so high that the station of the city Chapala was flooded and had to be abandoned. Today, flooding would be less likely because the water level of the lake has dropped due to the extraction of drinking water for the nearby city. Currently, the relatively shallow lake also suffers from eutrophication and has to be repeatedly cleaned of water hyacinths. The once flooded railway station now houses a museum.

Merida and the art academy

Merida once had one of the most beautiful train stations in Mexico. After passenger traffic in the station ended in the 1990s, the station building now shows itself in its old splendor. In 2007, an art academy moved into the newly renovated building. Merida is the capital of the state of Yucatan and once had a huge, unique network of 4500 km, mostly horse-drawn trams. Most of these trams opened up sisal plantations and connected them with cities and train stations. When synthetic fibers were developed in the 1920s, sisal production declined rapidly, many of the plantation railways were closed down, and soon the same fate befell interurban and inner-city railways.

Queretaro and the altar

The Querteraro station was built in the French style by an English company and inaugurated in 1903 by the president himself, Porfirio Diaz. In the station, there is an altar for railway workers who lost their lives. Although the city no longer has any passenger rail transport, freight trains still run here, and there are still deaths when shunting.

Tapachula and the death train

Tapachula, in the state of Chiapas, is the southernmost metropolitan area in Mexico. It has a population of about 320,000. From here, it is only a few kilometers to the border with the poor neighboring country Guatemala. From Tapachula, freight trains travel north to the US. Many migrants from Guatemala and other Central American countries are attracted by this. They cross the border illegally here, jump on the freight trains at night in the station of Tapachula, hoping to be transported to the US border. Many fall off the trains and are injured, disabled, or even die. This is why the trains leaving Tapachula are also known as the "Death Trains." In 2005, Hurricane Stan devastated the region, including the railway infrastructure, bringing the flow of rail migrants to a temporary halt.

Guatemala City- Estación Central

In the 1770s, a series of earthquakes and volcanic eruptions destroyed the old capital of Guatemala, now called Antigua Guatemala. The ruins of the earthquake can still be found there today. A careful search for a safe location for a new capital was carried out, and it was found in a valley whose topography seemed to indicate that earthquakes were rare there. The new capital was called Guatemala City. Nevertheless, in 1917, an earthquake occurred, which destroyed the main train station, among other things. After that, a safer and lighter wooden station was built for the passengers, but it burned down in 1973. When the third station was built, there was no longer any particular motivation for the design. A simple flat brick building was erected, where little could collapse or burn down. Today, this structure is more endangered by demolition than by natural catastrophes, because scheduled rail passenger transport no longer exists in Guatemala. After all, there is a railway museum in the station today.

The station copy

The old railway station of Guatemala City, which was destroyed by the earthquake, has been restored as a copy. A replica of the station was built in the amusement park *Xetulul*, which opened in 2002, and a train, the park railway of Xetulul, stops at it again. Since the rebuilt station is located at the entrance to the park, more people than ever before pass through the old station. And somehow, visitors must feel like they are in Lindau (Bavaria), because in Xetulul, a few steps from the station, there is a replica of the Lindau harbor tower.

Quetzaltenango

The city of Quetzaltenango (180,000 inhabitants) is proud to have been the starting point of the only electric railway line in the country: the *Ferrocarril de los Altos.* This spectacular railway line was 44 km long and connected Quetzaltenango with San Felipe (not far from San Felipe is the Xetulul amusement park). Originally, it was to be built as a rack railway because the difference in altitude between the two terminals is almost 2000 m. However, it was finally decided to build a friction railway but with electric propulsion. Opened in 1930, the railway was built by Krupp and AEG. Yet, already in 1933, landslides caused the track to collapse. In Quetzaltenango, which once had boarding halls and extensive parking facilities, the railway has not yet been forgotten. A railway museum has been set up in the former railway station, and a memorial plaque at the station reminds of the former electric railway line.

Zacapa

Since 1896, Zacapa has been a railway junction in eastern Guatemala. Here, the railway line to El Salvador branches off the Guatemala City-Puerto Barrios line. However, only freight trains and occasional tourist trains now pass the station. Additionally, this traffic is interrupted again and again by landslides and in recent times by rail theft. When the scheduled passenger traffic in Zacapa closed in the 1990s, the office equipment of the station, with its dial telephone and mechanical typewriter, was so outdated that it was directly turned into a museum. The station was once connected to a hotel where the Chilean Nobel Prize winner for literature Gabriela Mistral (1889-1957) stayed in 1930. Today, it is part of the museum, and Mistral's room still features the original décor.

3.3 Nicaragua

On 31 December 1993, the railway service in Nicaragua was discontinued. Several factors contributed to this, including the country's impoverishment after the civil war and the Sandinista rule, and the then conservative government followed a market economy course and was not willing to subsidize the railways. In addition, the country was ruled by President Violeta Chamorro (1990-97), and women are usually less railway freaks than men.

⊙ Niquinohomo

The Nicaraguan guerrilla leader Augusto Sandino, who was born in 1894 in a house near the train station in the village of Niquinohomo-Later Sandino, traveled a lot by train. In 1920, for example, he had to leave Nicaragua after a shooting, and he took the train to La Ceiba, Honduras, to work in a rum warehouse. He also traveled by train in Guatemala. Today, there are plans to establish an Augusto Sandino Museum in the disused station of Niquinohomo.
The airport of the Nicaraguan capital Managua is already called Augusto Sandino Airport, although Sandino had never traveled by plane from there.

⊙ Leon and the poet

Leon has one of the oldest railway stations in Nicaragua. It was built in 1882, and it was the first building in the city where steel was used for the roof truss. In 1907, the station became part of the country's literary history. The national poet Ruben Dario took a train ride from Corinto to Leon and wrote the book *Journey in Nicaragua: A Tropical Intermezzo* about his travels. In 1979, the rather unadorned railway station suffered damage during the civil war. Today, a market has settled in the station, and trains have not stopped here for a long time.

Granada and the school

Once, the cities of Leon and Granada competed for the capital function of Nicaragua. As a compromise, the town of Managua, located in between, was finally made the capital in 1858. However, while Managua was completely destroyed by an earthquake in 1972, Leon and Granada retained their historical architecture, including their railway stations. The red-and-white painted station of Granada, built in a strange neoclassical style in 1888, was once one of the most beautiful station buildings in Central America and today houses a school.

Managua

Once, Managua had a stately station, which resembled the one in Grenada with its architecture and its barrel roof. However, the heavy earthquake in 1972 and economically difficult decades after that took their toll. During the term of President Enrique Bolanos (2002-2007), the remains of the building were finally demolished. A mini-slum has now spread out over the wasteland where the capital's railway station once stood. A capital city dweller commented in a blog that a president from Managua would have treated the architectural heritage with more respect and that Bolanos would not have tolerated the demolition of the railway station in his home town of Masaya.

Masaya

And indeed, Masaya has a station, unlike Managua. It was built in 1932, and the station makes a harmonious impression with its arcade arches. Given its central location in the city, which was once a railway junction and grew around it, it is to be renovated and converted into a cultural center.

Panama - the first transcontinental railway

Surprisingly, the *Panama Railway*, opened in 1855, was the first transcontinental railway line. A US company built the line because Americans, in particular, were interested in avoiding the shipping traffic detour around the southern tip of South America. Even before the opening of the Panama Canal, the railway made it possible to transport goods largely by sea from the American east coast to the west coast. Despite its length of only 77 km, the construction of the railway was difficult, and 12,000 people are said to have died. Today, the railway is also important for tourism. A train departs daily from the station of the Pacific city of Panama City to Colon on the Atlantic Ocean. By the way, this trip is actually east to west because the Atlantic terminus of the line is located more to the west than the Pacific terminus. Surprisingly, the tracks in Panama City station have the same gauge as those in Russia, but this is not a coincidence. The 1524 mm wide gauge (5 feet) was the standard in the southern states of the US around 1840(the Panama Railway was built by Americans), and the US engineer George Washington Whistler also implemented this gauge on the St. Petersburg-Moscow line.

San José (Costa Rica)

In autumn 2005, a limited suburban train service was introduced in San José, the capital of Costa Rica, linking the country's largest university (35,000 students) with the Estación del Pacifico central station and an industrial area. During the first days, the train ride was free as an incentive to get to know the railway. From Pacifico station, a tourist train, the *Tico Train*, also runs on Saturdays and Sundays to the neighboring town of Caldera. However, the country lives up to its nickname of "Central America's Switzerland" through another railway: the *Swiss Railway*. It is a 3.5 km long 600 mm light railway built by a Swiss in the 1990s. It today belongs to the Hotel *Los Héroes* in Nuevo Arenal.

Cartago (Costa Rica)

In 2008, the wooden railway station of the city of Cartago, which was built around 1900 and is under monumental protection, was renovated to be used as a cultural center from then on. The Roman motto "Carthage must be destroyed" probably did not apply here.

La Ceiba (Honduras)

The city of La Ceiba, located on the Caribbean coast, was once the only city in Honduras where rail passenger transport still existed until 2010. Every half hour, a train leaves the city center on a 1067 mm line to the eastern part of the city, which is only 3 km away. For the trip, all that is needed is a locomotive and a converted freight car without side walls. There are, therefore, no train crossings, and only a minimum of personnel is required. The Honduras railways were once built by American banana companies as narrow-gauge (Cape-gauge) lines in order to access important banana-growing areas from the coast. Hurricane Mitch in 1998 destroyed much of the country's rail infrastructure. However, La Ceiba retained its small railway line.

San Pedro Sula- reactivation with simple means

In September 2010 in San Pedro Sula (Honduras), railway tracks were cleared of debris and garbage, ties were built by the staff from wooden beams, and missing rail sections were replaced in order to set up a rail service between the main station and the long-distance bus terminal with two old passenger cars and a locomotive every 30 minutes.

3.5 The Caribbean

Villanueva- Cuba's former railway station

Cuba was a (Spanish) colony longer than other countries in Latin America but had its first railway line quite early. From 1837 to 1912, a train ran from Villanueva station in the capital to the suburb of Bejucal. This was the first train in Cuba, and it existed 12 years before the first one in the mother country Spain. The reason for this was the export interests of the sugar cane growers.

The main station of Havana

Havana's double-towered main station, built in 1912, looks Cuban with its Spanish neo-renaissance style. However, it was built by US architects, and the style may even have been modeled on the old Atlanta station, which was later demolished. At one time, the station even had the American flag next to the Cuban flag.

☞ Havana's La Coubre station is named after a French cargo ship that in 1960 exploded in the city's harbor with 76 tons of ammunition onboard (over 100 dead).

Havana Casablanca and the Hershey Railway

Although Havana's Casablanca station is only a bus stop and you have to take a ferry from the city center to reach it, this simple station is still frequented by foreign tourists. The *Hershey Electric Railway*, the only electrified railway in Cuba, departs from here. It was built in 1921 by *Hershey*, the American chocolate company that owned sugar cane fields and a sugar mill in Cuba, with a station called Hershey. However, the sugar mill was closed in 2002, and since then, many railway enthusiasts have been worried about its survival.

The sugar cane railway of St. Kitts

Sugar was once considered a kind of white gold. In the 18th century, the Caribbean developed into an important sugar cane growing region, which was fought over between European colonial powers. The sugar island of St. Kitts was ,at times, the richest British colony. However, when it became possible to produce sugar on a large scale from sugar beet, the price of Caribbean sugar began to fall. Sugar producers, therefore, attempted to remain profitable through rationalization. In Basseterre, the capital of St. Kitts, a sugar factory was built in 1912. Additionally, in 1926, a narrow-gauge railway was built around the island to transport the sugar cane to the factory. While the sugar cane cultivation was stopped long ago on other Caribbean islands, in St. Kitts, it lasted until the third millennium. Yet, in July 2005, the last narrow-gauge freight train drove into the factory yard, and the machines in the factory were shut down. However, in 2003, the newly founded private *St. Kitts Scenic Railway* had begun to run tourist trains on the narrow gauge railway. Today, the tourist trains run daily on a 30 km stretch of track from Basseterre to La Valle station and combined with bus sections, travel around the island. The former sugar cane railway is now called the "Last Railway in the West Indies."

The Kendal train accident

One of America's worst train accidents (254 deaths) occurred on an island where there is no rail service at all today: Jamaica. On a Sunday in September 1957, a diesel train with 12 wooden passenger coaches was on its way back from Montego Bay to the Jamaican capital Kingston. In addition to regular passengers, mostly members of a Catholic travel group, numerous pickpockets had boarded the train in Montego Bay. With 1600 passengers, the train was completely overcrowded. Shortly before midnight near the village of Kendal, the driver signaled with three shrill alarm sounds that he had lost control of the train, a few minutes before it derailed. Over 200 passengers lost their lives, and 700 were injured.

San Juan, Puerto Rico

Puerto Rico once had a railway network of 500 km, which made the coastal areas very accessible. San Juan, the capital of the island, had a stately two-winged station with a clock tower in the middle and trams on the forecourt. But after the Second World War, road competition with the railways quickly led to a decline, and as early as 1953, rail passenger transport on the island was discontinued. San Juan's railway station fell into disrepair; windows were smashed, the tower lost its clock, and finally, demolition excavators arrived.

The Jimenez railway station

Elections were held in Puerto Rico on 7 November 1944. Train number 3 departed from San Juan to Ponce that day with many passengers who traveled to their home communities to vote. The train stopped at Jimenez station and routinely changed drivers with the oncoming train. However, the new driver had experience with freight trains,but had never driven a passenger train. At 2 a.m., the train with its six wagons left the station to go down into a valley. But the train was going too fast, and it eventually derailed down in the valley. The locomotive crashed into a ditch, and a freight car pushed into a passenger car. Sixteen people died, making this the worst rail accident in Puerto Rico's history.

4. South America

In South America, there is only little long-distance rail passenger transport with a few lines remain mainly for tourism. Buses dominate long-distance transport, while air travel is also important in Brazil, which has an extensive territory. Countries with (modest) long-distance rail transport include Peru, Chile, and particularly, Argentina (about 8 billion passenger-kilometers per year), which once had a dense railway network. In Venezuela, oil money has helped to re-establish a modest long-distance rail network, and a similar situation is emerging in Ecuador. However, earthquakes, tropical storms, and landslides repeatedly cause setbacks in many countries.

Argentina and Brazil are the only countries in Latin America that are considering building high-speed rail lines (Buenos Aires-Cordoba, São Paulo-Rio de Janeiro), but there is little concrete progress on such plans.

Rail freight transport is important in Brazil. The country has large ore deposits, and new rail lines are even being built to transport ore. In the south of the country, agricultural goods (coffee, soybeans) are also transported by rail to the export ports. Due to urbanization and increasing traffic jams, rail transport in cities is now booming. In the meantime, suburban railways are being expanded in larger agglomerations, and the railways are moving back into the surrounding area. The remaining railway stations in the big cities are also benefiting from this. Buenos Aires is the best place to speak of an existing railway station culture. Additionally, São Paulo still has magnificent stations, which are, however, only used for local traffic by suburban trains.

There are also beautiful stations in the big cities of Colombia and Chile.

4.1 Colombia

Due to its difficult topography, Colombia has never been a major railway country. Important cities of the country, such as Bogota, Medellin, and Cali, are located in the mountains and on different elevations, which makes it difficult to overcome great differences in altitude and to have a railway connection. The railway history of the country is nevertheless interesting. It begins in 1855, in Panama, with the world's first transcontinental railway line because Panama was then still part of Colombia. It was not until the 1880s that the first tracks of present-day Colombia were laid in the port of Barranquilla. As the Rio Magdalena was the main transport axis for a long time, it took until the 1950s for a small, coherent railway network to be established in the country. Yet, a few decades later, passenger traffic was already being shut down. The security situation, with rebel troops controlling large parts of the country, put an end to rail passenger transport in the 1990s. Today, there are only a few tourist train routes left, but an expansion of rail transport in the Bogota region is planned. Despite the small size of the railway network, there are interesting station buildings in the big cities, especially in Bogota and Medellin.

Bogota-Estación de la Sabana and the pigeons

The representative central station of Bogota, *Estacion de la Sabana* (Sabana means savannah, which is where Bogota lies), which only has one tourist train on Saturday and Sunday, has different references to the bird world. On the one hand, the neoclassical style of the entrance building, completed in 1924, is crowned by a huge condor. This is the heraldic bird of Colombia. While the English architect William Lidstone designed the building, an American architect named Adler (Eagle) was responsible for the railway facilities. The front of the station building again offers landing places for pigeons, which, however, settle at a suitable distance from the stone condor. And pigeons also have to do with Colombia because the country is named after the American discoverer Columbus, and in Latin, Columbus means pigeon.

Bogota- Usaquen

From Bogota Sabana station, tourist trains leave for the weekend via the suburban train station Usaquen to Zapaquira, where there is a salt cathedral to visit.

Usaquen station is reminiscent of a small-town train station in Switzerland, with its neat green and white paint scheme, the height indication on the façade, and the flower boxes in front of the windows. However, the architectural model for the station was actually Belgian provincial stations. And because it is wedged like an island between two streets in front of a shopping center, it is somehow a typical American station.

Medellin

Colombia's few railway lines did not grow into a coherent network until the 1950s (when it was torn apart again by closures) because, for a long time, they were oriented towards the river Rio Magdalena as the main transport axis. Moreover, important towns in the interior of the country are located on different mountain ranges and could only be connected by rail by overcoming great differences in altitude. Thus, Medellin was not connected by a railway line until 1914, although it was built in a French neoclassical style. However, it was already closed in 1981. Today it houses an art museum.

⊙ Cali

On August 7, 1956, seven trucks of the Colombian army loaded with 42 tons of dynamite exploded at the old train station of Cali for reasons never explained. More than a thousand people died in the explosion, and the station building was completely destroyed. The new station building was decorated with numerous murals by the local painter Hernando Tejada (1924-1998) and is, therefore, a listed Colombian national monument.

Manizales

The Colombian town of Manizales, situated in a coffee-growing area on the eastern slope of the Central Cordilleras, once had the longest transport cableway in the world. The coffee had to be transported over a mountain ridge to the river port of Mariquita, more than 2000 meters below. Since the First World War was raging, one of the supporting masts built in Europe did not arrive because the transit ship was sunk by a German submarine. In 1916, the cable car was opened. At times, the cable car was even used for passenger transport. In Manizales, a listed mast still reminds us of the former means of transport. Today, cable cars are experiencing a renaissance in Colombia. In Medellin and Manizales, cable cars are now used as a means of local transport.

Manizales did not receive a railway station until the 1920s. Since the coffee boom provided the necessary means to build the station, the splendid building design had to show the wealth of this period. Somehow, the station resembles the Julio Prestes station of São Paulo, which was likewise conceived during the coffee boom times. However, Manizales' station was only connected by a branch line, and soon rail traffic was going downhill anyway. Today, there are no tracks at the station, and a university has been established in the station building.

⊙ Aracataca and Garcia Marquez

The famous Colombian writer Garcia Marquez was born in the small town of Aracataca. In his books, he immortalized the city as Macondo. Aracataca also has a small train station where no scheduled trains have stopped for a long time. However, in May 2007, an old train, "the yellow train from Macondo," rumbled through the coastal province and stopped in the station for a long time. On the train were Garcia Marquez and his wife Mercedes Barca, who waved out the window. Marquez lives in Mexico City and had not been to his home town for 25 years. However, 2007 was declared Marques Year in Colombia, and the writer was invited to his home country.

⊙ "Train of Ice and Fire" in the station of Aracataca

More than a decade before Marquez's return trip, the station of Aracataca had illustrious guests. In 1993, the French band Mano Negra, founded in 1987, was on tour in South America. In Colombia, they wanted to make a sign of hope in the country torn apart by violence. Manu Chao, the band's lead singer from Spain, had the idea of traveling the country with a group of artists in a converted passenger train and giving free concerts to the population at the stations along the way. In the port city of Santa Marta, the starting point of the railway line to Bogota, they started their journey. Yet by the time they arrived in Aracataca, the group of about 100 musicians, acrobats, and artists largely disbanded, and Manu Chao had to continue the journey to Bogota with only a handful of determined people.

4.2 Venezuela

The left-wing populist government under President Hugo Chavez liked to spend oil money on public projects that caught the media's attention. After all, the railways also profited from this, and Venezuela, which was never a large railway country, now has some railway lines again, at least as far as local urban transport is concerned. The inner-city traffic also profited from new underground and light rail lines. Currently, Venezuela is in a deep economic crisis, halting the construction of new lines.

Caracas Simon Bolivar railway station

The Caracas-born independence fighter Simon Bolivar (1783-1830) is considered a national hero, almost a national saint, in Venezuela. The currency is called Bolivar, the country calls itself Bolivar Republic since 2001, and a portrait of Bolivar can be found in all offices.

Therefore, it is not surprising that when a new suburban train connection to Cua (41 km away) was opened in 2006, the new terminus in Caracas was named *Freedom Fighter Simon Bolivar Station*. The Caracas train station is not the only station on the line which refers in its name to Bolivar and his life. Another station on the line to Cua was named after Bolivar's school teacher Don Simon Rodriguez.

Barquisimetos Transbarca

The city of Barquisimeto in the west of Venezuela will also soon have a Simon Bolivar station. Yet, there is not even a connection to the rail network there. However, this is under construction, as is the large intermodal central station Transbarca, which will link rail transport with the urban trolleybus system.

4.3 Brazil

State of São Paulo

São Paulo Estacão da Luz - the British railway station

São Paulo is situated on a high plateau that drops steeply to the coast. Therefore, the first railway line to the port of Santos had to be equipped with cogwheels. It was designed by a Scottish engineer and operated by a British company: *São Paulo Railways* (SPR). The terminal station of the line in the da Luz district of São Paulo, opened in 1901, was also built by the British. All materials, even the screws, were imported from Scotland. In September 1946, the railway company was nationalized. Shortly before that, the station building and the SPR archives inside burned down. Arson is suspected and an interest of the SPR in destroying sensitive documents.

São Paulo da Luz Station (Photo: Wikipedia)

112

São Paulo Julio Prestes - the French station

The fact that the construction of the station da Luz was exclusively done by the British hurt the national pride of the Brazilians. Thus, when another railway company - the Sorocabana Railway - was planning a station in São Paulo, they wanted to surpass da Luz station with a French-style building constructed by Brazilians. The clock tower was also planned to be even higher than that of the competitor. The new New York stations Grand Central and Penn Station provided additional inspiration, and the coffee boom provided the necessary financial means. Construction finally began in 1926 not far from Luz Station, but in 1929, the world economic crisis meant that the project had to be scaled back. The planned massive barrel copper roofs were never realized, and the station ended with a flat roof. The large inner courtyard was left completely without a roof, and it rained on the palm trees placed there. By the time Julio Prestes Station was finally opened in 1938, the railway era had already passed its peak and competition from motor traffic and airplanes became increasingly fierce after the war. In the 1990s, all of Brazil's long-distance rail traffic was finally closed, and the Julio Prestes station became just a local railway station. The magnificent interior design with columns, coffee plant ornaments in the window, and floor mosaics led to the decision to preserve the station for cultural use. After a total renovation, a concert hall,reputedly the best in South America, was built for the symphony orchestra of the São Paulo State Opera House. A complex sound insulation system with rubber bedding and triple glazing ensures that performances are not disturbed by railway noise.

São Paulo Estaçao Bras (Roosevelt Station)

São Paulo has an English-style station (da Luz), a French one (Julio Prestes), and finally, with Roosevelt Station, it got an American Art Deco station. However, after alterations, not much remained of the original style. Today, Roosevelt is part of the Bras station complex, which with its brutalist concrete architecture can almost be considered a typical Brazilian station. Due to its connection to an important subway line, Bras is probably the most frequented railway complex in Brazil today.

Santos

Allegedly, Victoria Station in London served as the architectural model for the station of Santos, which lies at the coastal end of the line towards São Paulo. Yet, it only roughly resembles the station in London. Otherwise, Santos station rather displays some French style elements.

Mauá - the first bicycle station in Latin America

Adilson Alcantara, the stationmaster of Mauá - a suburban train station in the São Paulo conurbation - observed that more and more bicycles were parked at the station. The excess of bicycles increasingly obstructed access to the station. In 2001, he, therefore, founded the *Ascobike Association* and set up a guarded bicycle park at the station for its members. Now, the first bike station in Latin America is well frequented with over 2000 users per day.

Paranapiacaba and the clock tower

In 1856, the British-owned *São Paulo Railway Company* was granted a concession to build a railway line from the port of Santos to the Jundai coffee-growing region located 70 km north of São Paulo. Paranapiacaba, 40 km southeast of São Paulo, was designated as the operating base. At times, more than 1000 workers were stationed here, including many British. It was the last station before a cogwheel track went steeply down the coast. The plateau, on which São Paulo is located (800 meters above sea level), is often covered in fog, and the climate is much cooler than on the coast. Therefore, the British must have felt at home here. The station tower, a replica of the Big Ben Tower of London, also contributed to this sense of home. There is nothing left of the station building today, yet, the strange Big Ben copy still stands at the tracks in Paranapiacaba.

Campos do Jordão and Abernessia

170 km northeast of São Paulo, at an altitude of 1628 m, lies the town of Campos do Jordão. Because of the healthy mountain air, a pulmonary clinic was opened here in 1874. Since transport on horseback was exhausting for the sick, a 47 km long meter-gauge railway was built from the valley town of Pindamonhangaba up the mountain between 1912 and 1914. Today, this small railway is mainly used by tourists. With a peak of 1743 m, it reaches the highest point of all of the railway lines in the country. Despite gradients of more than 10 percent, no racks are used. The Abernessia station is located on the line. This name is a combination of the Scottish city names Aberdeen and Inverness since the investors for the construction of the railway came from Scotland. In Campos do Jordão itself, the cool mountain climate, the half-timbered houses, the railway infrastructure with trams, light railways, and the station contribute to the appealing feeling for Brazilian tourists that they are already a little bit in Europe.

Campinas and the church

The architecture of historic railway stations often resembles that of church buildings. The Campinas station building, built in 1872, even seems to have a church set directly into its façade. In the 1980s, the church's blessing might have been needed, as the metal canopy over the platform collapsed after one of the pillars was brought down by a protruding bar of a badly loaded passing freight train. Today the station building houses a cultural center, and the last passenger train left the station in 2001.

Caieiras and the Russian Tsar

Caieiras is a city in the state of São Paulo, whose station is connected to the São Paulo suburban rail network. Built in 1897, the station was once part of the England-owned *São Paulo Railway*. At one time, a cable car used to leave the station to transport limestone. As the British also built the station at that time, it displays many English style elements, such as the cast-iron columns of the platform roofs.

In the city, the following story is often told: the English once wanted to sell the station to the Russians, but the Tsar had no money. So, it came to Brazil.

Brasilia's little used train station

The relocation of the capital function from Rio de Janeiro to Brasilia was the life's work of Brazilian president Juscelino Kubitschek. It was preceded by a vision of the Italian priest Don Bosco (later canonized), who had dreamed that a futuristic city would emerge in the hinterland of Brazil. The city planner of Brasilia was Lucio Costa (1902-1998), and the chief architect was Oscar Niemeyer (1907-2012). Brasilia was built between 1956 and 1960 in only 41 months, had the layout of an airplane, and was from the beginning, a car-friendly city (the city only got a subway in 2001) with its wide streets and separation of the functions of living and working, as provided for in the Athens Charter.

The construction of the Brasilia railway station, designed by Oscar Niemeyer, did not begin until a decade and a half after the city was inaugurated. The station was opened in 1977, but by that time, the Brazilian railways were already in decline. In the early 1990s, the last passenger train left the station. Today, the station reflects the traffic situation in Brazil: freight trains still leave here (rail freight traffic in Brazil is significant and growing), while passenger traffic is handled by a bus station at the station building.

Goiania and the Art Deco station

Not far from Brasilia is the city of Goiania, the capital of the state of Goiás. Perhaps Brasilia would never have existed if Goiania had not been founded in October 1933 as a completely new planned capital of the state. The first buildings in the city were influenced by the Art Deco style prevailing at the time and are now listed as historical monuments. One of these buildings is the city's railway station with its striking clock tower, built in 1950 and closed in the 1980s.

Rio - Central do Brasil

The main station of Rio de Janeiro, Central do Brasil, was on everyone's lips in 1998. That year, the film *Central do Brasil* by Brazilian director Walter Salles (*1956) was released in cinemas with great success. It is about a former teacher who runs a writing office for illiterate people at the train station, but the teacher never sends these letters.

Rio - Estaçao de Maua

In addition to the Central do Brasil Station, Rio had another terminus station, the Leopoldina Station, which was built in 1926. This station was later named Baron Maua Station after the builder of Brazil's first railway line, constructed in 1854 between Rio and Petropolis and served by the station. In 2001, however, passenger traffic ended at the station, and the station building was closed in 2004.

Belo Horizonte and its station tower

Belo Horizonte (Brazilians also call it BH or Beaga) was originally called Curral Del Rey and later Cidade de Minas, prior to the city adopting its current name. The city also had several railway station buildings. In 1895, when the town was still very small, there was only a small wooden building. This was finally replaced at the beginning of the 20th century by a station building with a neo-gothic tower, which carried the city's first public clock, and was similar to Prague Town Hall. In 1922, a new station building with a smaller tower but a wider building in the Baroque style was inaugurated. This building still exists today, but now it hosts an art museum. Today, more trains than ever pass the station, as the city railway line has been extended to a suburban railway.

Blumenau - the half-timbered station

The town of Blumenau, founded by German immigrants in 1850 under the leadership of pharmacist Hermann Blumenau, was once so influenced by German culture that even the railway station was built in the half-timbered style. However, the station building was later replaced by an inconspicuous little house with hints of the Art Deco style. The building is now used as a residential building. However, some hints of German culture remain in Blumenau: the world's largest Oktoberfest outside Munich.

Rolandia's changing name

The city of Rolandia in the state of Parana is also shaped by German immigrants. In 1936, a railway station was opened. At that time, the city was still called Caviuna. Soon after, the town grew due to Germans who had escaped from the Nazi regime, and the station and town were renamed Rolandia. Due to the Second World War atrocities, Germanness was not so well regarded in Brazil anymore, and the city was renamed Caviuna again in 1943. Finally, in 1947, its name switched back to Rolandia. In 1957, Bremen coffee entrepreneurs donated a replica of the Bremen Roland statue to the town. The city's 1930s train station, which saw many renames in a short time, has since been replaced by a small, inconspicuous concrete station, which has no name at all.

Porto Velho and the Madeira-Mamoré Railway

In order to develop Bolivian rubber plantations, a railway line, the Madeira-Mamoré Railway, was built from 1907-

119

1912 along a section of river at the Rio Madeira in the west of Brazil. This section of the river was not navigable due to rapids and waterfalls. More than 3000 people died during its construction, hence the nickname *Devil's Railway*. Yet, only one year after its opening, the project became economically inefficient due to the decline in rubber prices and the construction of a line from Bolivia to the Pacific Ocean. In 1972, this isolated railway operation, which was not connected to the rest of the network, was finally shut down. In 2000, a landslide also brought the remaining Sunday steam train tourist traffic to a standstill. Since then, the railway station area has become a focus of crime and prostitution, and railway vehicles have been sold. However, Brazilian and international associations of railway enthusiasts are campaigning for it to be reopened as a museum railway.

Cachoeira

Cachoeira is a city on the Paraguaçu River in the state of Bahia. Since the city center is close to the river and there is no bridge to Saõ Felix on the other side of the river, the station was originally designed as a terminus station. Yet, one day a bridge was built, which led into the station forecourt and where rails were also laid. How was it possible to connect the rails at the back of the station with the bridge, given the limited space? Finally, a solution was found: a hole was drilled through the front of the station building, allowing trains to pass through the station to reach the forecourt and the bridge (a turning maneuver is, however, necessary).

4.4 Andean countries

Lima Desamparados

The train station of Lima is named *Estación Desamparados* - in English train station of the helpless - after the former Jesuit convent Nuestra Senora de Desamparados. Some German stations could also be called that, if all ticket counters are closed and the vending machines do not work well. However, in this station- -which is also used as a cultural center - there are no ticket machines, as only a tourist train leaves once a week for the Andean city Huáncayo. Additionally, there is now only one track, so it should not be much of a problem to find the right train.

Unlike in the other Andean countries, the 364 km long track is in standard gauge. In the 1850s, the Polish engineer Malinowski had made bold plans for a railway to the Andes. The income from the export of guano fertilizer suddenly provided Peru with the necessary funds, and the American entrepreneur Henry Meiggs had the determination to see the project through. Meiggs said, "wherever Llamas run, I can lay tracks."

Galera, the high station

Galera station in Peru, which is on the Central Andean Railway, is 4781 m above sea level and was once considered the highest in the world. Today, however, there is a station in Tibet at 5068 m above sea level. From 1992-2003, the station was out of service because the terrorist group *Sen-dero Luminoso* was active in the area.

The railway station of Machu Picchu

The spectacular Inca city of Machu Picchu can best be reached by train. Ninety-two percent of the annual 400,000 visitors to the site travel from Cuzco on the 914 mm narrow-gauge train Bingham Express. This line is named after the American archaeologist Hiram Bingham (1875-1956), who discovered the ruined city. Visitors are taken by bus up the mountain from the Puente Ruinas train station.

Quito-Chimbacalle

In June 1908, America Alfonso, daughter of President Eloy Alfaro, hammered a golden nail into the last meter of the track at Quito-Chimbacalle station. The railway line built from the coastal city into the Andes had finally reached the Ecuadorian capital at an altitude of over 2800 meters. But the rail traffic was not particularly intensive. Only three times a week, a train went to the coast. On the occasion of the 100th anniversary of the opening, the station was renovated in 2008 and renamed Eloy Alfaro Station. A bust of Alfaro was also erected. A special feature of the station is the turning loop. The platform is on the side of the loop, and trains can enter and leave the station without changing locomotives.

Riobamba and the Devil's Nose

On the now interrupted railway line from Quito to the coast, there is also the famous "Devil's Nose" with its four hairpin bends. This section of the track is used by tourist trains from Rio Bamba station (2754 m) via Alausi (2360 m) on the mountain to the valley station Sibambe (1806 m). This section was once considered the "most difficult railway line in the world."

Punos railway ferry

In Peru, there was once even an international rail ferry, which was designed for two gauges.

The starting point on the Peruvian side was the city of Puno on Lake Titicaca. The standard gauge tracks from the Peruvian hinterland arrived there. In Guaqui on the Bolivian side, however, the railway traffic continued in meter gauge.

La Paz, Estación Arica

Bolivia suffers from the trauma of multiple territorial losses to stronger neighboring states. Particularly painful for the Bolivians was its lost sea access to Chile in 1904. Even today, soldiers are still being trained in Bolivia for a non-existent navy. However, Chile committed itself to facilitate Bolivia's access to the sea by expanding the Arica-La Paz railway line. In La Paz, the Arica railway station was opened in 1913. Yet, the traffic volume has decreased in recent years. In the spring of 2008, it was decided to close the station, which was required renovation and convert it into a museum.

Santa Cruz de la Sierra

Surprisingly, the relatively poor Bolivia is one of the few Latin American countries that still have long-distance rail transport. The city of Santa Cruz de la Sierra even has a modern combined rail and bus station (bimodal Terminal), opened in 2001. From the city's train station, there are even connections in two directions: to the east (Brazil) and to the south (Argentina). However, the tracks are so bad that the train from Santa Cruz to Quijarro on the border with Brazil is also known as the "death train."

4.5 Uruguay and Paraguay

Montevideo - the nostalgic railway station

Montevideo, the capital of Uruguay, is sometimes referred to as *BA* (Buenos Aires) *minus LA (*Los Angeles and its urban sprawl). Uruguay has only 3 million inhabitants, and although forty percent of the population live in the agglomeration of Montevideo, the city is not a juggernaut like other Latin American metropoles. Its structures are more reminiscent of a European city. Montevideo also has one of the most beautiful main train stations in Latin America, a building that resembles a French castle. There is even train service in the station, which is not usually the case in the region. However, the station is becoming more and more dilapidated. Certain construction industry interests have pushed through the idea that a new station building should take over the transport function of the centrally located station in order to free up the track field for real estate projects, including high-rise buildings. However, the population depends on the old station, and the new Apeardo station, built 500 m away from the old one in an everyday architectural style, only went into operation after a delay. The reasons for the delay were the diameters of the track curves were too small and the tracks were too close to the platforms. It is quite possible that the plans for laying the tracks were secretly sabotaged by the railways, given the sentimentality surrounding the old station.

Asuncion's neo-gothic station

The beautiful neo-gothic central station of Asuncion was built in 1856. The railway traffic was never particularly intensive, only one line (Asuncion-Encarnacion) was in operation throughout the country. Today, the Asuncion railway station houses a railway museum.

4.6 Chile

Caldera

In the small town of Caldera in the north of Chile, the first railway station in South America was built in 1850. The goal was to develop local deposits of sodium nitrate (Chilean saltpeter was, at that time, an important fertilizer). The station still exists, as it was restored in 1999, and now serves cultural purposes today. However, no trains have left from here for a long time. The station was part of the Caldera-Copiapó line, opened in 1854, which was of great importance for the development of the mineral resources of the Atacama region. The railway line was built on the initiative of the American William Wheelwright, who founded the *Pacific Steam Navigation Company* and was commercially active in Chile. He even commissioned plans for a railway from Valparaiso, Chile to Buenos Aires, Argentina. However, the Chilean government rejected the plans as too risky.

Copiapó

The station of Copiapó, which was opened in 1854, and is located at the terminus of the line, still exists. After its restoration in 1982, it housed a railway museum. It was closed in 1998, yet, two steam locomotives can still be seen in the station square.

Santiago Alameda Station

An example of the French influence on the railway station architecture of South America is, besides Montevideo, the central station of Santiago de Chile, the Alameda station. The station was built in 1885 (the first station in Santiago was opened in 1857). The French company Schneider built the station, the station concourse was designed by Gustave

Eiffel, and the two side buildings are reminiscent of miniature editions of the Parisian Arc de Triomphe. Now it is the home of shopping centers. The railway station, which is also connected to the city's underground network, continues to provide rail transport. From here, trains depart south to San Fernando every quarter of an hour and to Chillán every hour.

Santiago Alameda-Bahnhof

⊙ Santiago Mapocho station

Santiago once had another long-distance train station, the Mapocho station. It was located on the river of the same name, and its architecture was inspired by the Paris Quai d'Orsay station. Since 1991, the station building has been home to a cultural center. In April 2009, the center was awarded the *Queen Sofia International Prize* for the preservation and restoration of cultural heritage by a Spanish development agency. The Chilean poet Pablo

Neruda (1904-1973) once even wrote an ode to the station. The text of this ode is on display in the entrance hall of the station. The ode ends with the words, "I love you, old station, you who lie by the murky river and the wild current of the Mapocho, you create with your passengers your own river of infinite love."

The names of railway stations south of Santiago are engraved in the wall of the station hall. The Mapocho station (see picture below), however, instead served the cities north of Santiago.

Valparaiso-Puerto

Unlike Santiago, the important Chilean port city of Valparaiso no longer has any long-distance rail transport. Transport to Santiago is by bus only. Therefore, former railway lines and stations have been integrated into a metro system (Merval), which was opened in 2005 and replaced the railways. Thus, the former port railway station *Valparaiso Puerto* became a metro station from where subway trains leave every fifteen minutes to the city of Limache, 43 km away. The metro runs largely above ground but goes underground in the neighboring town of Vina del Mar. The first underground station (from which nothing can be seen) is called Miramar (meaning "view of the sea").

The miners' station of Sewell

The former mining town of Sewell (named after the US American Barton Sewell, President of the *US Braden Copper Company*), situated at 2000 m in the Andes, was once one of the few places in South America that could only be reached by train. From the train station, the inhabitants transported their belongings with ladder wagons to their houses on the mountainside. The village once had the largest underground copper mining site in the world. After the end of mining, Sewell - which had 15,000 inhabitants at the height of its development - is now practically extinct. Since 2006, however, the town has been on the UNESCO World Heritage List, and its railway station, once so important to the population, is protected.

James Bond and the Baquedano railway station

In the spring of 2008, filming for the new James Bond film *Quantum of Solace* took place at the train station in the small Chilean town of Baquedano. As they were filming, Carlos Lopez, the mayor of the town, suddenly raced into the scene with his car and almost ran over part of the film crew. His car finally came to a halt between Bond's car and the film camera. This was not an accident, but rather intentional. The mayor of this northern Chilean city was very angry about the fact that a scene that was supposed to take place in Bolivia was shot in his town.

Buenos Aires-Constitución and the riots

In contrast to other Latin American metropolises, Buenos Aires can certainly still call itself a railway city. There are several terminal stations, which still have dense suburban and even long-distance traffic. Additionally, Buenos Aires has an extensive subway network, and once, the city had one of the largest tram networks in the world with over 850 km. With 600,000 commuters daily, the Estación Constitución, built in 1907 by British architects (in the French style), is the busiest station in the city. In 1925, the Prince of Wales, who was on a state visit, laid the foundation stone for the station extension. Thanks to the British, the tracks in the station have the same gauge as those in Kolkata. In the 1850s, locomotives, originally destined for India, were used by England in the Crimean War and then sold cheaply to Argentina, where the railway network was developed in Indian 1676 mm wide gauge. In May 2007, commuter unrest broke out here after train delays.

Buenos Aires - Once de Septiembre

Another important station is Once de Septiembre (meaning the September 11th station), which is intended to commemorate the anniversary of the death of Argentine President Domingo Faustino, who died in 1888. Since 2001, however, this date no longer has a good ring to it, especially among US citizens, who are increasingly discovering Buenos Aires as a film location.

Buenos Aires-Retiro and the tower

The Retiro Station, built in 1915, is an important long-distance train station in Buenos Aires (actually, there are three separate station buildings here). The steel parts of the main building, including the platform halls, were manufactured in Liverpool and were transported by ship to Argentina. The architecture of the station was modeled on buildings in Cardiff, Wales (notably the city's town hall) and London. The National Museum of Wales, which was built later, also resembles the Retiro station.

In front of Retiro Station stands the 76 m high *Torre de los Ingleses*, built in 1916. The tower was a gift from the British, whose king could not travel to the country's centenary celebrations in 1910. After the Falkland War between Argentina and Great Britain in 1982, the neo-renaissance tower was renamed *Torre Monumental*. However, the capital city people still say "English Tower," although the name does not quite fit either, as the symbols of England (rose), Scotland (thistle), Wales (dragon), and Ireland (cloverleaf) are attached to its four sides.

⊙ From La Plata to Tibet

The Austrian mountaineer and geographer Heinrich Harrer (1912-2006) set out on a Himalayan expedition in 1939 with the aim of climbing Nanga Parbat (the so-called "Schiksalsberg der Deutschen," or "mountain of destiny for the Germans"). After the outbreak of the World War, the British arrested Harrer in India as for being a German citizen, their current war opponent. Yet, he managed to escape to Tibet, where he stayed for seven years and became the teacher of the present Dalai Lama. In 1997, Heinrich Harrer's book *Seven Years in Tibet* was filmed with a budget of 70 million dollars and Brad Pitt in the leading role. One scene of the film takes place in the main train station in Graz, where Harrer says goodbye to his sworn wife Ingrid and sets off on a journey to Asia with Mr. Aufschnaiter as the head of the expedition. However, this scene was not filmed in the Graz train station because it is only sixty years old. The old station was destroyed during the war. Instead, the station of the Argentinean city of La Plata had to serve as Graz's main railway station. Additionally, parts of the film were shot in Argentina because the mountains looked similar to those in Tibet, and the production costs were low. When they were looking for a station location, they found one in the Buenos Aires suburb of La Plata. The station building there looked vintage enough to resemble the train station of Graz. Since then, the station building has been shut down and converted into a museum. Trains still run to La Plata.

Rosario Norte and Rosario Central

Once the long-distance station of the city, Rosario Norte is now the only station in Rosario that still has (low) passenger traffic. During the so-called "golden age" of the Argentinean railways between 1935 and 1940, more than 300,000 passengers departed here every year (800 per day). At the beginning of the 1990s, the Menem government privatized the railways. The new private companies were only interested in profitable freight transport, and long-distance passenger transport was largely shut down. However, there are now daily passenger trains again between Rosario and Buenos Aires.

Rosario Central

Rosario Central - the former central station of the city - with its clock tower in the style of Italian neo-Gothic is one of the most architecturally remarkable stations in South America. The station was closed in 1977, but later it was declared a protected building and renovated. However, the tracks were removed. Now, offices of the regional administration are located here.

Rosario Antártida Argentina ('Argentine Arctic')

Another architecturally special station in Rosario is located in the Fisherton district. The originally named Fisherton station was built in the 1890s by a British company in the British style. When the Argentinean railway network was nationalized in 1948, the station was renamed *Antártida Argentina* because Argentina claims an Antarctic segment.

The name of the Malvinas station (the Argentinean name for the Falkland Islands) in the Buenos Aires area also expresses a territorial claim.

Salta la Linda

Because of its well-preserved historical architecture, the 1187 m high city of Salta in the west of the country is also called *La linda*, meaning the beautiful. Salta's railway station also makes a good impression. From here, the tourist train *Tren de las Nubes* (cloud train) departs, which climbs up to 4220 m. Until 1981, there were even passenger trains from Salta to the port city of Antofagasta in Chile.

Trelev and the Welsh

Around 1860, the Welsh nationalist Michael D. Jones had the idea of creating a new "little Wales." Observing that Welsh people were rapidly integrating in English-speaking countries such as the USA and Australia, he proposed the establishment of a Welsh-speaking colony outside the English-speaking world. Patagonia was eventually chosen because it was remote, and Argentina wanted to provide land along the Chubut River. In 1862, the Welshman Lewis Jones set out for Patagonia to see if the area was suitable for Welsh emigrants. The ship first entered the port of Buenos Aires, where the Home Secretary confirmed the deal. However, on its way further south, a storm pushed the ship into a bay, which they named Porth Madryn (now Puerto

Madryn) after a property in Wales. On their return to Wales, they declared the area to be very suitable for Welsh colonists. In 1865, a ship carrying 153 settlers reached the mouth of the Chubut River, where the town of Rawson was founded. As the mouth of the Chubut River was not very suitable for a harbor, it was decided to build the *Central of Chubut Railway* from Puerto Madryn to the Chubut Valley. Lewis Jones was the main initiator of the railway. In 1866, a ship with 400 settlers and equipment for the railway construction arrived in Puerto Madryn. At the Chubut end of the railway line, the village Trelew was founded, whose name is a combination of the Welsh word for town (Tre) and Lewis Jones' first name. Trelew received a railway station in 1889, which shows British architectural influences. The station, which has long since been shut down, now houses the Pueblo de Louis Museum, also named after Lewis Jones.

Ushuaia - the end of the world

The city of Ushuaia (64,000 inhabitants) on the island of Tierra del Fuego in southernmost Argentina is nicknamed the "End of the World." At one time, prisoners were brought to this inhospitable plain, and a large prison was built for this purpose in 1902. A 600 mm narrow-gauge railway was built for the transport of material, which initially ran on wooden rails (a Xilorail). In 1909, the first trains of this "prison railway" were running. The station belonging to it is thus also the southernmost station in the world. In 1952, the "prison railway" was closed. However, as Ushuaia was becoming more and more a tourist destination, the railway was reopened in 1994 for tourist purposes as "Tren del Fin del Mundo" (Train at the End of the World). There are even plans to extend it towards the city or to create a connection with a new tram line.

Annex

1. Remarkable/most beautiful stations
Appearance in lists of different publications

Station/source	1	2	3	4	5	6	7	Insg.
New York Grand Central	x		x	x	x	x	x	6
London St. Pancras	x	(x)		x	x			4
Bombay CST*		x	x		x	x		4
Helsinki Main station	x	x		x				3
Antwerpen CS		x			x			2
Lahore Station (Pakistan)	x				x			2
Milano Centrale				x		x		2
Washington Union Station				x			x	2
Los Angeles Union Station			x				x	2
Philadelphia Gravers Lane		x						1
Toronto Union Station			x					1
Buenos Aires Retiro		x						1
St.Louis Union Station							x	1
Cininnati Union Station							x	1
Chicago Union Station							x	1
Kansas City Union Station							x	1
30th Street Station Philad.							x	1
Old Penn Station New York							x	1

Bold: Multiple mentionings, ( ) Parts of the station * World heritage

1. J. Glancey im *The Guardian* of 23. 11. 2006 (6 Bahnhöfe)
2. Mark Irving `1001 Buildings you must see before you die´, Cassel Illustrated, London 2007
3. Richard Cavendish (Hrsg) `1001 Historic Sites you must see before you die´, Cassel Illustrated, London 2007
4. Brian Solomon `Railway masterpieces´, 2002
5. Newsweek 19 Januar 2009, Routes Less Traveled, List of 9 best stations
6. Other lists: <u>UNESCO-World heritage</u>: Bombay CST, the US-Architect <u>Frank Lloyd Wright</u> counted Milano Centrale and New York Grand Central among the most beautiful stations in the world
7. Stations on the list, America's favourite Architecture".
The list was set by the American Institute of Architects in 2007 by showing 2000 Americans, photos of 247 buildings selected by architects. Grand Central Terminal in New York reached rank 13, Washington Union Station rank 37.

2. Architectural models of stations

Station	Model (partially)
USA	
New York (old) Penn Station	Brandenburg Gate (outside) Caracalla Baths (inside)
New York Grand Central	*Inside, partially:* Paris Gare d´Orsay
Newton Kansas Railway Station	Shakespeare´s house in Stratford-upon -Avon
Richmond Union Station	Pantheon (Rome)
Seattle King Street (Tower)	Campanile of Venice
St. Louis Union Station	Carcassonne (Walls and towers)
Washington Union Station	Arch of Konstantin/Rome (outside), Diokletian-Baths (inside)
Canada	
Ottawa Union Station	General: New York Penn Station Caracalla-Baths (inside)
Quebec Gare du Palais	Chateau Frontenac (Quebec)
Latin America	
Mexico City Buenavista	Roma Termini
Havana (Cuba) Estacion Central	Old station of Atlanta? Hotel Flagler Florida?
Santos (Brazil)	London Victoria Station
Paranapiacaba (Brazil)	Tower: Big Ben, London
Santiago de Chile Main station	Side building: Paris Triumph Arch

3. The largest stations according to the number of passengers (partially including subway and local traffic) in Thousand, working days, around 2015

Country	Station (1000 travellers and visitors per day)
USA	<u>New York</u>: Grand Central Terminal 750 (200 transit, 550visitors and subway passengers); Penn Station 600 (of which 30 Amtrak), <u>Chicago</u> Union Station 126 (of which long distance 6), Ogilvie Transportation Centre 38 <u>Other cities</u>: Boston South Station 52, Washington Union Station 11 (only long distance), Los Angeles Union Station 4 (long distance)
Canada	Toronto Union Station 200 Of which rail: 130 (Via: 8, GO Transit 150), subway75). Montreal Gare Central 50
Mexico	Mexico City Buenavista: 90 (local transport)
Brazil	São Paulo Est. da Luz 180, Rio de Janeiro Central 350 (incl. subway)
Uruguay	Montevideo 1.2
Argentina	<u>Buenos Aires</u> (incl. subway): Constitucion 600, Once 400, Retiro 300

4. Important Amtrak stations in the US

Passengers in million (without visitors)

Station	Million Passengers		
	2009	2011	2018
New York Penn Station	7.83	9.00	9.86
Washington Union Station	4.28	4.85	5.04
Philadelphia 30th Street	3.68	3.87	4.42
Chicago Union Station	3.08	3.39	3.29
Los Angeles Union Station	1.48	1.61	1.45
Boston South	1.29	1.36	1.53
Sacramento Valley Rail Station	1.11	1.18	1.07
Baltimore Penn Station	0.93	0.95	1.03
Albany Rensselaer Station	0.72	0.77	0.79
San Diego Union Station	0.73	0.75	0.67
New Haven Union Station, CT	0.66	0.74	0.69
Wilmington	0.66	0.72	0.70
Penn Station Newark, NJ	0.63	0.68	0.70
Portland, Oregon	0.62	0.67	0.57
Seattle	0.62	0.67	0.68
Baltimore Washington Airport	0.62	0.66	0.75
Providence Station	0.58	0.63	0.76
Milwaukee Intermodal Station	0.55	0.62	0.60
Emeryville, CA	0.52	0.58	0.59
Harrisburg Transportation Center	0.54	0.54	0.51

Other railway companies (Local transport)

Station	Company	Mio Passeng.
Grand Central Terminal (NY)	Metro North	67 (2018)
Pennsylvania Station (NY)	NJT	27.3 (2017)
Boston South	MBTA	7 (2012)
Newark	NJT	9.5 (2017)
Hoboken Terminal	NJT	5.5 (2017)
Toronto (Canada)	VIA	2.9 (2012)
	GO Transit	69.5 (2015)

5. Comparison Amtrak (USA)-Via Rail (Canada)(2018)

Company	Amtrak	VIA Rail
Passengers (million)	31.7 (2018)	4.74 (2018)
Growth (year before) %	+5.1	+8.0 %
Network length (km)	34 411	12 500
Of which own tracks (km)	1006	223
Employed persons	20 000	3115
Stations	500	121
Passenger coaches	1543	431
Locomotives, rail cars	484	73
Trains per day	300	72
Revenue (bliion $)	3.4	0.37 (CDN$)
Cost coverage (operation)	71%	57%

6. Railway networks in the Americas (km), 2014-18

Country	Total	Broad gauge	Normal gauge	Narrow gauge
USA	293 564	-	293 564	-
Canada	77 932	-	77 932	-
Argentina	36 917	26 391	2 745	7523
Brazil	29 850	5 822	194	23 342
Mexico	20 825	-	20 825	-
Cuba	8 367	-	8 195	172
Chile	7 282	3 428	-	3 854
Bolivia	3 960	-	-	3 960
Columbia	2 141	-	150	1 991
Peru	1 854	-	1 730	124
Uruguay	1 673	-	1 673	-
Ecuador	965	-	-	965
Guatemala	800	-	-	800
Honduras	699	-	-	699
Venezuela	447	-	447	-
Costa Rica	278	-	-	278

Source: CIA World Factbook (consulted July 2019)

Broad gauge: 1676 mm: Argentina, Chile, 1600 mm: Brazil

Normal gauge:1435 mm Narrow gauge: 1067 mm: Ecuador; Costa Rica, 1000 mm: Brazil, Argentina, Boliva, Chile; 914 mm: Columbia, Peru, Guatemala

Literature

Bund Deutscher Architekten (Hrsg.)
Renaissance der Bahnhöfe
Vieweg Verlag, Braunschweig 1996

Günter Feuereißen
Dampf über Südamerika
Gondrom, München, 1990

Kevin J. Holland
Classic American Railroad terminals
MBI Publishing Company, Osceola 2001

Mark Irving
1001 Buildings You Must See Before You Die
Cassel Illustrated, London 2007

Anthony Robins, New York Transit Museum
Grand Central Terminal
ABRAMS, New York 2013

Ralf Roth
Das Jahrhundert der Eisenbahn
Jan Thorbecke Verlag, Ostfildern 2004

Brian Solomon
Railway Masterpieces
David &Charles, Newton Abbot 2002

Wolstan Webb
Thirty years around the world
Nyons, 1991

Joe Welsh
Die Eisenbahn in den USA
Transpress, Stuttgart 2007

Karl Zimmermann
Ageless Grand Central kicks off its second century
In Trains February 2013, Seiten 41-49

Webssites, a) general

Wikipedia (Seiten zu verschiedenen Bahnhöfen)
www.de.wikipedia.org

America's Favourite Architecture
http://www.favoritearchitecture.org/

Amtrak
www.amtrak.com

Anecdotage.com (Amerikanische Anekdotenwebseite)
www.anecdotage.com

CIA World Factbook
https://www.cia.gov/library/publications/the-world-factbook/index.html

Ferrocarriles Suburbanos (Mexiko Stadt)
http://www.fsuburbanos.com

Infrastructurist
http://www.infrastructurist.com/2009/06/22/11-beautiful-train-stations-that-fell-to-the-wrecking-ball/

Mexlist
http://www.mexlist.com/welcome.htm

Estacoes Ferroviárias do Brasil
http://www.estacoesferroviarias.com.br/

Via Rail (Kanada)
http://ourcompany.viarail.ca

UIC (International Railway Union (Paris)
http://www.uic.asso.fr

Urbanrail
http://www.urbanrail.net

World´s Largest and Busiest Rail Stations
http://www.skyscrapercity.com/showthread.php?t=342415

b) Specific stations

Ann Arbor Observer (Ann Arbor Michigan Central Depot)
http://www.aadl.org/aaobserver/15258

University of Michigan (Besuch Tafts)
http://www.umich.edu/whitehouse/presidents/taft.html

Decatur (Illinois)
http://www.haunteddecatur.com/railroads.html

Triple Threat Blues band Library
http://www.triplethreatbluesband.com/wchandy.htm

Gary Indiana
http://www.lostindiana.net/html/union_station.html

Granada (Nicaragua)
http://www.manfut.org/granada/c-estacion.html

Bahnlinie Caldera-Copiapó in Chile
http://www.geovirtual.cl/Museovirtual/FFCC/tur190Caldera01.htm

Library and archives Canada
Anekdote: The prime minister and the newspaper boy
http://www.collectionscanada.gc.ca/2/4/h4-3182-e.html

Niles depot lighting
http://user.mc.net/~louisvw/depot/Niles_Lights/nilesLights.htm

Santa Fe Depot (San Diego)
http://www.sdrm.org/sfd.html

St. Thomas (Canada)
http://www.railwaycapital.ca/history_station

Zacapa (Guatemala)
http://www.xplorandoguatemala.com/viajando/museo-del-ferrocarril-en-zacapa.htm

Persons contributing with comments and suggestions: Frank Stenvall (Malmö), Jörg Berkes (Langen).

Other railway statioin books of Richard Deiss

The Palace of a thousand winds and the Gooseberry station
Short stories on 222 plus 2 railway stations in Germany
Books on Demand, Norderstedt 2020

The destiny station beyond the mountains
Short stories on 111 railway stations in the Alpine countries
Books on Demand, Norderstedt 2020

Cathedral of the winged wheel and sugarbeet station
Short stories on 111 railway stations in the Alpine countries
Books on Demand, Norderstedt 2020

Der Lebkuchenbahnhof am Ende der Welt
Kleine Geschichten zu 222 Bahnhöfen in Afrika, Asien und
Ozeanien, Books on Demand, Norderstedt 2011

Worcester Union Station